Kota Kinabalu

Kota Kinabalu

and Surrounding Areas

Wendy Hutton

Opus Publications
Kota Kinabalu

2010

Published by:

Opus Publications Sdn. Bhd. (183100-X)
A913, 9th Floor, Wisma Merdeka Phase 1,
P. O. Box 15566, 88864 Kota Kinabalu, Sabah, Malaysia.
Tel: +6088 233098 Fax: +6088 240768
e-mail: info@nhpborneo.com Website: www.nhpborneo.com

Kota Kinabalu and Surrounding Areas *by* Wendy Hutton
ISBN 978-983-3987-40-5

First published August 2010.

Design and layout by Chan Hin Ching.

Half-title page: The coastline stretching north of Kota Kinabalu, in Tuaran district, with a golf course at the right of a meandering river.
PHOTO BY PEIN LEE/STB

Frontispiece: The city is just minutes across the bay to Gaya island and other islands of the Tunku Abdul Rahman Park.
PHOTO BY PEIN LEE/STB

Contents page: Right on the South China Sea at Pantai Dalit, the luxurious Rasa Ria Resort is adjacent to a Golf and Country Club and Spa.
PHOTO BY RABANI AYUB/STB

Contents

1.
Where it all begins

The first glimpse of Sabah for many visitors is the dramatic view from the plane as it approaches the airport of Kota Kinabalu, the state capital. As the plane reduces height, rice fields, scattered villages, a small coastal town and a lazy river or two spilling out into the South China Sea may come into view. Beyond the long string of sandy beaches, the occasional island is a smudge of green on a deep blue backdrop, while inland, beyond the rice fields, forested hills rise abruptly. With any luck, the awesome granite mountain after which the city is named might be glimpsed as the plane prepares to make its descent.

Suddenly, the plane is flying over suburbs or over the city itself, before coming in to land just 10 kilometres from the city centre. Beyond the gleaming new International Terminal building, Kota Kinabalu and the rest of Sabah await.

One of the 13 states which make up the modern nation of Malaysia, Sabah — once known as British North Borneo — is still very much the embodiment of Borneo, with its astonishing variety of plants, wildlife and ethnic groups. Some visitors come in search of adventure, such as white-water kayaking, mountain biking, scuba diving or climbing to the summit of Mount Kinabalu. Others prefer to focus on bird watching or native orchids of rare beauty, while some visitors opt for sun, shopping and seafood.

World-renowned locations such as the Sepilok Orang Utan Rehabilitation Centre and prime dive spots including Sipadan and Lankayan islands are on Sabah's east coast. However, Kota Kinabalu and its environs have a wide range of attractions to enchant and excite. There are rainforests, mountains and fast-flowing rivers; islands with sandy beaches and coral reefs; rice plains and swamp forests which are home to Borneo's strange Proboscis Monkey; quaint villages and contemporary shopping malls; ritual observances and nightclubs; luxurious resorts with spas and golf courses, and village home-stays where a whole new way of life can be experienced.

This book offers an insight into Kota Kinabalu and its surroundings, places which can easily be reached on a day trip by visitors staying in the city (although many of these spots merit at least one or two nights' stay). Major places of interest in Kota Kinabalu and the rest of the West Coast District are included, ranging as far north as Kota Belud and east to Kinabalu Park, and to part of the Interior District, including Beaufort and the Klias Peninsula.

Opposite: Protected from the South China Sea by Gaya island (with a private resort seen in the foreground), the small settlement of Jesselton grew up around its port, gradually stretching along the coastline to eventually become the city of Kota Kinabalu.
PHOTO BY LEE YEN PHIN

—

Following pages: With a waterfront resort complete with marina and golf course located just south of the city centre (left), and protected by islands, Kota Kinabalu enjoys an idyllic location.
PHOTO BY LEE YEN PHIN

—

Right: The green-roofed buildings of the Federal Government complex are adjacent to the beautiful campus of Universiti Malaysia Sabah.
PHOTO BY C.L. CHAN

—

Right, below: The "Double Six" memorial to the late Tun Fuad Stephens, then Sabah's Chief Minister, and other cabinet ministers who died in a plane crash on this site on 6 June 1976.
PHOTO BY C.L. CHAN

—

Opposite: This striking tower, Menara Tun Mustapha, home of the Sabah Foundation or Yayasan Sabah, stands at the edge of Likas Bay.
PHOTO BY LEE YEN PHIN

—

Following pages: Kota Kinabalu and its suburbs are cradled between the forested mountains of the Crocker Range and the sea.
PHOTO BY PEIN LEE/STB

—

2.

From Jesselton to Kota Kinabalu

Kota Kinabalu today is so proudly confident in its role as the capital of Sabah that it is somewhat surprising to learn that the city achieved its position by a series of historical mishaps.

During the 19th century, dreaming of the riches that might be gained in the largely unpopulated island of Borneo, a number of Western adventurers cast their eyes eastward. With James Brooke already installed as the first White Rajah of Sarawak in 1841, attention turned further north. The Sultan of Brunei (who held nominal control over all of northern Borneo) ceded the island of Labuan off southwestern Sabah to the British Crown in 1846. Subsequently, in 1865, the Sultan granted an American trading company a lease at Kimanis (south of Kota Kinabalu), and the company founded the settlement of Ellena in 1865.

When this settlement failed within a year, the lease passed through several hands, eventually finishing up with a trading company which was granted a Royal Charter from the British Crown. The so-called Chartered Company named their territory — gained, as was the norm in those imperialistic days, without any consent from the natives — British North Borneo. Kudat on Borneo's northwest tip was chosen as the capital in 1882. However, despite its good natural harbour, Kudat did not have a reliable supply of fresh water so a couple of years later, the capital was moved across to Sandakan on the east coast.

Previous pages: Rice paddies and vegetable farms can often be seen when approaching Kota Kinabalu International Airport from the south.
PHOTO BY PEIN LEE/STB

—

Opposite: This pre-war photograph shows the Court House on the hilltop behind the Atkinson Clock Tower (still standing), with other buildings located alongside the railway station.
PHOTO COURTESY OF MAX H. HILCKES/ NICHOLAS K.M. TAN

—

Following pages: The large building on the left in this 1950s' photograph, the town's first cinema, still stands today, although the stilt village behind (Kampung Air) has long been reclaimed.
PHOTO COURTESY OF NICHOLAS K.M. TAN

—

With the British colonial penchant for islands (think Labuan, Singapore, Penang and Hong Kong), their first west coast settlement in North Borneo was established in 1882 on Pulau Gaya, the large island opposite today's Kota Kinabalu. A few Bajau fishermen were already living here and on other islands in Gaya Bay. When the officials of the Chartered Company arrived on Pulau Gaya, these Bajau were soon joined by a few Chinese shopkeepers and traders. The new settlement progressed slowly until fate intervened in the shape of a Bajau rebel leader, Mat Salleh. Resenting the imposition of foreign control, Mat Salleh burned the Gaya settlement to the ground in 1897, forcing the Chartered Company to seek a new location.

A strip of flat land on the mainland opposite Pulau Gaya was selected, and the new settlement named Jesselton after Charles Jessel, a director of the Chartered Company. (Somewhat ironically, the swampy coast near Jesselton was known to the locals as Api Api, after the mangrove trees lit up by fireflies at night; *api* is also the word for "fire", the reason for the British moving here.)

Jesselton was linked with British North Borneo's other settlements (Kudat, Sandakan and Tawau) by sea, the forest-covered mountains of the interior being an insurmountable challenge until the latter part of the 20th century. Rubber estates were established to the north and south of Jesselton, and Chinese immigrants started market gardens and small trading operations.

The construction of Borneo's only commercial railway made a huge difference to the fortunes of Jesselton. To enable the transport of rubber and agricultural produce grown in the fertile interior plains, the Chartered Company began building a railway line to the west coast. This was to lead via Beaufort to the port of Weston (named after the man responsible for the railway, Arthur West) on Brunei Bay. Chance once again favoured Jesselton when it was discovered that Brunei Bay was too shallow for commercial ships and the Weston port had to be abandoned. Tanjung Lipat at Jesselton provided the perfect alternative deep-water port, and thus the railway line linking it with Beaufort was completed in 1902.

Jesselton was a small settlement of wooden houses and administrative buildings, built on stilts above the ground for coolness, or perched over the shallow reefs on the coast. These water villages or *kampung air* remained a distinctive feature of Jesselton for the next century, with a few vestiges still existing into the beginning of the 21st century.

The large open green space or Padang at the base of Signal Hill (so named because it was used as a navigation point for shipping) became a popular recreation ground, with the British and locals each establishing their own sporting clubs. Games of cricket and rugby, as well as race meetings, were the major entertainments of the early days, especially for the foreigners living in Jesselton.

Above: The rebuilding of Kota Kinabalu, after the destructive bombing at the end of WWII, continued well into the 1950s.
PHOTO COURTESY OF NICHOLAS K.M. TAN
—
Following pages: The building on the far left is now the home of Sabah Tourism; in 1953, when this photograph was taken, it was right at the edge of the bay; now, owing to reclamation, it stands three blocks back from the sea.
PHOTO COURTESY OF NICHOLAS K.M. TAN
—

The main street of Jesselton was Bond Street (now Jalan Gaya), with Beach Street (Jalan Pantai) running along the coastline. Successive reclamations of the shallow reefs have continued until today, pushing the coastline further and further towards Pulau Gaya and greatly increasing the amount of flat land available for construction.

Life in Jesselton proceeded uneventfully until the Japanese invasion in January 1942. Allied prisoners-of-war were held in Sandakan and locals who tried to help them suffered terrible deprivations for the next three years. The Chinese were often brutally treated by the Japanese, and in 1943, a group led by the Chinese but including men from all major ethnic groups staged a rebellion known as the Jesselton Uprising. This failed, however, and the leader, Albert Kwok, was executed by the Japanese early in 1944, along with 175 others. (The site of their murders, at Petagas, is marked with a memorial and the event commemorated each year.)

Above: This photograph taken 100 years ago shows Jesselton Railway Station, with the Court House on the hilltop to the right.
PHOTO COURTESY OF NICHOLAS K.M. TAN

In 1945, the Australian Armed Forces led an invasion to oust the Japanese from Borneo. To dislodge the Japanese and destroy any support they might have, Sandakan, Jesselton and the island of Labuan were heavily bombed by the Allies. After the Japanese surrender, Sandakan was in ruins, with not a single building left standing in the heart of the town, with Jesselton faring only slightly better.

Massive reconstruction was required throughout North Borneo. Lacking the resources to carry out this task, the Chartered Company handed North Borneo over to the British Crown, and in 1946, it became a colony. Because of the total ruin of Sandakan, it was decided that the capital should be transferred to Jesselton on the west coast. Thus Jesselton, initially established because of a fire in the Chartered Company's Gaya Island settlement, became the capital of North Borneo as a result of war damage to Sandakan.

Little by little, the rebuilding of the new capital progressed, with the first group of post-war shop houses in Bond Street (which remain until today) officially opened in 1954. Jesselton remained a small town, with around only 20,000 residents in the 1950s.

Under post-war colonial rule, British North Borneo saw a period of considerable development. The improving economy (which received a boost from the Korean War of 1950–53 and the resulting boom in the price of rubber and other commodities) led to a slowly improving infrastructure and a better standard of living. Roads gradually pushed beyond Jesselton and air services linked the capital with Singapore and Malaya.

The push for independence in colonies around the world at the end of the war saw British North Borneo being granted its independence in 1963. It was renamed Sabah, with the town of Jesselton remaining as the capital. Moves to form a political alliance consisting of Malaya (independent since 1957), Sarawak, Sabah and Singapore resulted in the formation of Malaysia on 16 September 1963, with a ceremony held on Jesselton's Padang to mark the occasion. (Singapore left Malaysia two years later.)

From Jesselton to Kota Kinabalu

Although a number of residents were reluctant to see the name of Jesselton changed, it was decided that the town's name should no longer commemorate a long-gone director of the Chartered Company. Jesselton therefore became Kota Kinabalu, the City of Kinabalu, in 1967, honouring the mountain which dominates the west coast landscape.

During the timber boom, which reached its peak in the 1970s and '80s, hardwood logs felled in the Interior were shipped via the port of Kota Kinabalu. However, the majority of timber was taken from forests in eastern and southeastern Sabah and exported via Sandakan, which experienced an economic boom surpassing that of Kota Kinabalu.

With the gradual improvement of the roads around Kota Kinabalu and the opening of the town's first five-star resort in the mid-1970s, tourism began to take off. In the past decade, the greatly increased number of direct flights from around Asia has resulted in a dramatic increase in the number of visitors.

The local population increased rapidly and by 2000, when Kota Kinabalu officially received city status, numbered around 300,000. The construction of resorts and hotels, golf courses, new airport terminals, commercial buildings, shopping complexes and flyovers to ease traffic congestion have all made Kota Kinabalu one of the fastest growing cities in Malaysia today.

From the somewhat drab uniformity of post-war reconstruction to a new era of optimism and increasing affluence, the city landscape is changing. Kota Kinabalu is not a historic city with imposing buildings from bygone days, but a new and energetic city set in a location of unrivalled beauty, between the mountains and the sea.

Kota Kinabalu's priceless waterfront, with its views of Gaya Bay and across to the islands of the Tunku Abdul Rahman Marine Park, is being spruced up and promenades where both locals and visitors can enjoy its beauty are being created. The planting of flowering shrubs along road dividers and in traffic roundabouts adds to the lush beauty of long-established giant trees which still cast their welcome shade.

Set by the waters of the South China Sea, embraced by a lush tropical environment and watched over by the mighty Mount Kinabalu, Sabah's capital is indeed a city which deserves its sobriquet, the Rainforest City.

Below: This historic photograph taken at the Jesselton Padang on 16 September 1963 shows Tun Abdul Razak, Deputy Prime Minister of Malaysia and the official representative of the Yang di-Pertuan Agong of Malaysia, at the Sabah Malaysia Celebration. He is witnessing the Swearing-In Ceremony of His Excellency The Yang di-Pertua Negara by the Senior Puisne Judge, Mr L.D. Smith.

PHOTO COURTESY OF DEPARTMENT OF INFORMATION SABAH

—

Following pages: Jesselton (seen here in 1911) grew up on flat land near the port at Tanjung Lipat; the railway line leading to the port is seen to the right of the road in the centre of this photograph.

PHOTO COURTESY OF SABAH MUSEUM

—

3. A Kaleidoscope of Cultures

The steady beating of gongs provides a hypnotic background as dancers clad in simple black, glide effortlessly on bare feet. The sombre colour of the women's homespun skirts and tunics is the perfect backdrop to exuberant gold-braid trimming, with necklaces of heirloom beads, heavy antique coins and silver bells attached to belts worn around the waist or hips adding individuality to every costume. Sleek black hair is adorned with clusters of flowers, dyed feathers or coloured rattan headbands, making the outfit of Kadazandusun dancers a feast for the eyes.

In striking contrast, Bajau dancers shimmer in pink, lime green or yellow satin, the men topping it off with intricately woven headgear. The women are the embodiment of an Oriental princess, their flowing tops adorned with a breastplate of beaten gold motifs stitched onto a black cloth. Their ensemble is topped off with dramatic headgear resembling a stylised golden boat with intricate dangling gold ornaments.

On festive occasions such as the Pesta Ka'amatan or Harvest Festival held each May, and Kota Belud's Tamu Besar in October, Kota Kinabalu's original inhabitants (together with ethnic groups from the rest of Sabah) offer a glimpse into the remarkable diversity of races and cultures to be found here.

Visitors to North Borneo in the 19th century often remarked on the remarkable ethnic diversity of its people, and deduced that the unusual tolerance they observed was a result of generations of living side-by-side in a multi-ethnic society. Spenser St John, the English explorer who accompanied Sir Hugh Low on his expeditions to Mount Kinabalu, noted that in the Kota Belud district, the Dusun and Bajau often lived in almost adjoining villages. Intermarriage was relatively common, with some individuals being a mixture of as many as four different ethnic groups.

Opposite: Monsopiad Cultural Village focuses upon the cultural traditions of the local Kadazandusun community.
PHOTO BY PEIN LEE/STB

Above: A woman returning from the rice fields near Kota Belud.
PHOTO BY WENDY HUTTON

—

Above right: Young Papar Dusun women wearing their distinctive hats; each sub-group of the Kadazandusun has its own style of costume and headgear.
PHOTO BY C.V. CHONG

—

Opposite: The folding of his woven headgear proclaims that this man is a member of the West Coast Bajau ethnic group.
PHOTO BY HENRY KY CHIN

—

The vibrant mix of people in Kota Kinabalu today is like a microcosm of Sabah itself. The magnet of a capital city, with its increased employment and educational opportunities, means that people from most of Sabah's 32 indigenous ethnic groups are now living here.

They are joined by non-indigenous Sabahans, predominantly the Chinese, most of whose ancestors migrated in the late 19th and early 20th centuries. There is also a small population of Sikhs, descended from men brought to Sabah as police or military during the days of British North Borneo. Other non-native peoples include descendants of Javanese workers brought in to labour on rubber estates and large numbers of more recently arrived Indonesians and Filipinos. In Kota Kinabalu, there is also a small number of Malaysians of southern Indian origin who have come from Peninsular Malaysia seeking work in Sabah since the formation of the Malaysia Federation in 1963.

洋参须
5.00
天花粉 桑白皮
甘松

A Kaleidoscope of Culture

Sabah's indigenous peoples have been subjected to rapid modernisation in recent decades, and certain cultural practices including the wearing of traditional clothing are no longer part of everyday life, except for a few older folk. However, it is still possible to witness the rich cultural heritage of Kota Kinabalu and its surrounding districts, not just at the many local festivals but also in the weekly markets or *tamu*.

It was estimated in 1858 that there were only around 300 people living in Gaya Bay, in fishing villages on the islands of Gaya and Sepangar. On the mainland, indigenous Dusun tribes had long been established south of Jesselton in Putatan and a few kilometres inland in the Penampang district.

Moving away from what is now Kota Kinabalu, various sub-groups of the Kadazandusun family still live in their original districts: the Lotud in Tuaran; the Dusun Tindal, Dusun Tabilung and Dusun Tempasuk in the Kota Belud region; the Dusun Tangara of Papar and the Dusun Tatana on the Klias Peninsula.

It is not an exaggeration to say that rice was the cornerstone of life for the agricultural Dusun (now officially known to as Kadazandusun, even though many still refer themselves as either Dusun or Kadazan). These people were described as "the great agriculturalists of the Territory" by early Western visitors.

Opposite: A traditional Chinese medicine shop in old Kota Kinabalu (KK Lama) still does good business.

—

Above: Many Chinese businesses pass from one generation to the next, such as this well-known herbal medicine shop in a suburb of Kota Kinabalu.

—

Following pages: Heirloom belts worn as part of the Kadazandusun costume often contain old coins and antique silver rings, a display of family wealth and prestige.

—

PHOTOS BY PEIN LEE/STB

Top left: Monsopiad Cultural Village is built where the famous warrior after whom it is named lived more than 200 years ago.
PHOTO BY C.L. CHAN

—

Above: Visitors are invited to try their skill at a local dance performed between clacking bamboo poles during the cultural show.
PHOTO BY PEIN LEE/STB

—

Right: Visitors join performers on the suspension bridge for a souvenir photo.
PHOTO BY C.L. CHAN

—

Opposite: The buildings at Monsopiad Cultural Village are all made of traditional materials such as split bamboo, seen flanking the entrance.
PHOTO BY PEIN LEE/STB

—

Their staple food was grown in paddy fields along the flat coastal plains, while inland, non-irrigated rice was grown on the steep hillsides. Every stage of the cultivation of the precious grain was marked by ritual observances, culminating in a ceremony to give thanks for a successful harvest and to safeguard the rice spirit until the next planting. Even though a small number of Kadazandusun are still rice farmers, the Pesta Ka'amatan or Harvest Festival is embraced by all, with celebrations around the West Coast throughout the month of May, with two days of rituals and fun climaxing the event in Kota Kinabalu on the 30th and 31st May.

Ceremonies associated with rice growing, as well as healing and communicating with the spirits of the departed, have traditionally been conducted by ritual priestesses known as *bobohizan*, who spent many years learning lengthy chants which were transmitted orally from generation to generation. The original animistic beliefs of Borneo's indigenous Kadazandusun held that natural objects such as trees, rocks and rivers all had a spirit. Thus, respect for their environment was an integral part of their culture.

The independent social structure of the Dusuns in the 19th and early 20th century — where each village was governed as a separate entity, overseen by a council of older men — contrasted with the social structure of Bajau and Irranun or Lanun tribes of the West Coast, who paid tribute to a Chief. The freedom of Dusun women to go about their everyday life and work in the fields without being guarded by men was remarked upon by early visitors.

With the conversion of most Kadazandusun to other religious faiths (predominantly Christianity), the old rituals are losing their importance and the ritual priestesses are literally dying out. Modern medicine is replacing ancient cures (although the art of therapeutic massage and use of herbal medicines can still be found), and it seems that the age-old knowledge of the ritual priestesses and, on occasion, priests, is doomed to disappear.

Remnants of traditional Kadazandusun life — apart from the dances, games and contests of the annual Pesta Ka'amatan — can still be seen. One of the best places for a glimpse of Kadazandusun culture is the Monsopiad Cultural Village, just 16 kilometres from Kota Kinabalu in the Penampang district (a stronghold of the Kadazans for several centuries). This "living museum" — devoted to keeping alive the cultural traditions of Borneo's largest indigenous group — is set on fertile land beside a river which was once an important route for transportation.

Monsopiad Cultural Village is named after the ancestor of the family which still safeguards the 42 skulls taken by Monsopiad, a renowned headhunter who lived here more than two centuries ago. Although the ancient practice of ritual head-hunting exerts a fascination for many, the traditional buildings, costumes, adornments, cooking utensils and other aspects of daily life are equally interesting and give an excellent insight into the Kadazandusun. There are also traditional games, dances, food and even a chance to sample a local delicacy, live sago grubs.

Above: At Mari-Mari Cultural Village, tourists are invited to try their skill at jumping on the traditional bamboo trampoline found in Murut longhouses.
PHOTO BY WENDY HUTTON

Above left: Among the many demonstrations at Mari-Mari Cultural Village is the making of rice wine, with free samples for all.
PHOTO BY WENDY HUTTON

Opposite: A performer dressed as a Murut warrior; this particular ethnic group was renowned for its fearless fighters and skilled hunters.
PHOTO BY PEIN LEE/STB

Above: Looking like necklaces, strands of yeast cakes are crushed and mixed with cooked glutinous rice to make the ever-popular rice wine.

—

Above right: Fresh ginger, most of it grown in the interior valley across the Crocker Range, and leafy greens are always on sale.

—

Opposite: Piles of dried prawns and other dried fish are essential flavourings for many local dishes.

—

PHOTOS BY PEIN LEE/STB

Another beautifully located place northeast of Kota Kinabalu, the Mari-Mari Cultural Village, showcases several of Sabah's ethnic groups including the Kadazandusun, Lundayeh, Murut, Rungus and Bajau. As well as seeing life-sized traditional houses and longhouses with everyday artefacts, and being entertained by local dances, visitors get a chance to try their hand at typical activities such as shooting a blowpipe, giving a tattoo (non-permanent), cooking Bajau cakes and sampling rice wine.

An ideal place to see the Kadazandusun going about their daily life is to visit the *tamu* or weekly market held every Thursday and Friday morning at Donggongan, the centre of Penampang district and around 12 kilometres from Kota Kinabalu.

This *tamu* has all the usual fresh tropical fruits and vegetables, dried and fresh fish, meat and the type of produce you'd find in any major market around Kota Kinabalu. In addition, special delicacies such as wild honey, heart of palm, various fern tips, wild mushrooms, a distinctive sour fruit added to soups and stews, live sago grubs and other fascinating produce can be found.

Strands of large white discs resembling beads are in fact dried yeast, used in making rice wine, while locally grown tobacco and the ingredients for a "betel nut chew" (lime powder, areca nuts and betel leaves) are also on sale. Medicine men sit on the ground on a mat, their strange pharmacopeia ranged around them as they call out the magical properties of their wares to potential customers crowding around. There are likely to be dried seahorses, the strange fungal tree growth known as an ant plant, as well as various bits of bark and leaves. A gong seller may be playing to demonstrate the sonorous tones of this vital local musical instrument, and older Kadazan women in traditional dress can usually be seen.

The *tamu* at Donggongan, like other local markets, is always full of the freshest fruits and vegetables, a truly colourful sight. PHOTOS BY PEIN LEE/STB

Essential ingredients for the betel chew (top) include fresh betel leaves, sliced dried areca nuts and lime powder. Fresh sweet corn is a year-round snack. PHOTOS BY PEIN LEE/STB

SABAH

Although their ancestors originated in the islands of the southern Philippines, some groups of Bajau have been established along the west coast from as early as the 16th century. The Bajau were regarded as "very expert fishermen", and lived in wood and thatch houses built on the edge of the Mengkabong estuary just north of Kota Kinabalu. The saltwater-impregnated roots of the *nipah* palms, which grew abundantly in the estuary, were gathered, dried and burned. The ashes were then boiled in water until they dried up, leaving a coarse, rather bitter salt which was used as a trading item and also for salting and preserving large amounts of dried fish.

Some of the Bajau moved north from Mengkabong, settling the fertile Tempasuk plain watered by rivers flowing down from Mount Kinabalu, while others established a few coastal villages. There were already villages of agricultural Dusun tribes in the Tempasuk region, and the newly arrived Bajau gave up their traditional fishing and turned to making a living from agriculture, growing rice and raising cattle and water buffaloes.

The Bajau race was described by a 19th-century visitor as "very independent, and no one appears to obey authority". Although they were Muslim, Bajau women (like the Irranun and Suluk women, also originating in the southern Philippines) were not segregated from their menfolk as in most other Islamic societies but "would often sit with the men and enter freely into the subject under discussion". They dressed in brightly coloured sarongs with jangling silver and brass anklets above their bare feet.

Opposite: Traditional woven hats from several different ethnic groups and ceremonial brassware are displayed beside beads and rings used to adorn costumes or worn on the body.

—

Above left: Dried husks are used as a wrapping for locally grown tobacco.

—

Above: The skin of ripe bananas in Sabah ranges in colour from green, golden to red, the length varying from tiny finger-sized bananas to giant fruit 35–40 cm in length.

—

PHOTOS BY PEIN LEE/STB

Borneo hardwoods have been used to build the *tamu*, an attractive and cool market place at Donggongan popular with city housewives as well as those living in Penampang district.

PHOTO BY PEIN LEE/STB

Above: A Kadazandusun woman netting for small fish in a flooded area just off a Penampang highway.
PHOTO BY WENDY HUTTON
—
Above right: A group of jovial Rungus women, wearing distinctive brass arm coils.
PHOTO BY DAVID KIRKLAND/STB
—
Opposite: Their skill with horses has earned the West Coast Bajau the nickname “Cowboys of the East”.
PHOTO BY DAVID KIRKLAND/STB
—

The favourite pastime of Bajau men was cockfighting, but they became most famous for their riding skills, reputedly “never making use of their own legs if they could possibly get an animal to carry them“. As well as riding small ponies as they went about their daily activities, they would even ride water buffaloes or cows. The Bajau saddle was made of wood, covered with thin cloth; Western-style stirrups were replaced by a rope with a loop in the end, through which the big toe was inserted.

Although the use of ponies is diminishing, the West Coast Bajau are still often called the “Cowboys of the East”, and skilful Bajau riders dominate the horse-racing scene in Kota Kinabalu. They come into their own on festive occasions, especially the annual Tamu Besar, when they dress in ceremonial trousers, jacket and headgear, adorn themselves with a special dagger and carry a riding crop. Their ponies are even more gorgeously dressed, draped in colourful fabric literally from head to tail.

All Bajau are Muslim, but both the language and cultural practices of the West Coast Bajau differ from those of the more recently arrived Bajau on Sabah’s east coast.

The Sunday *tamu* held at Kota Belud is an ideal occasion to meet and mingle among the Bajau, as well as Irranun, Dusun from the Tempasuk plain, Rungus from up north, and Dusun hill folk who have come from afar to trade.

While the Kadazandusun and Bajau are the largest ethnic groups on the West Coast, other groups whose home is here include the Irranun (their ancestors, once known as Lanun) who hailed from Mindanao island in the southern Philippines), the Bisaya and two groups originally from further south in Brunei, the Bruneian and Kedayan (both groups living in the Beaufort district south of Kota Kinabalu).

4. Exploring the City

The sleepy settlement of Jesselton — its wood and thatch buildings straggling along the edge of Gaya Bay, perching over reefs or nestling on the lower slopes of Signal Hill — has been transformed into one of Malaysia's fastest growing cities in little more than a century.

Jesselton began life as an administrative outpost, and its few imposing buildings that eventually arose were obliterated by bombing at the end of World War II. Thus, the "Rainforest City" is not a place of historic monuments and grand colonial architecture. In fact, some of the towering shady trees on the hill behind the oldest part of the city are probably older than any of its buildings.

Offering the usual conveniences and comforts of a fast-modernising city, Kota Kinabalu is an ideal base for exploring its amazing hinterland. The city faces the islands of the Tunku Abdul Rahman Marine Park (see Chapter 5), with beautiful beaches, reefs and sea sports just moments away. The UNESCO World Heritage Site of Kinabalu Park, with Sabah's iconic mountain, can be reached in less than a couple of hours, as can the botanical wonders of the Crocker Range (see Chapter 6).

Those in search of wildlife will find it on Kota Kinabalu's outskirts at the Lok Kawi Wildlife Park, in bird sanctuaries right in town and also on the Klias Peninsula, where the unique Proboscis Monkey is a major attraction (see Chapter 7). Adventure lovers can thrill to everything from white-water rafting to mountain biking, or golfing to rock climbing on one of Southeast Asia's tallest mountains (see Chapter 8).

But what of the city itself? There are plenty of places where a one- or two-hour stroll offers an insight into local lifestyles; where great food can be enjoyed at inexpensive food centres or famous seafood restaurants; and where bargains can be found on a mat spread in front of a Rungus tribal woman sitting on a pedestrian bridge in the heart of town, or in an air-conditioned shopping mall selling international brands or intriguing souvenirs.

Opposite: Huge shady trees, some perhaps almost as old as KK itself, grow at the edge the city green or Padang Merdeka, and on Signal Hill, backing the commercial and banking district.
PHOTO BY CHAN SHUK LING

—

Following pages: A gateway marks one end of Gaya Street, once the city's main road and the site of a very popular Sunday market.
PHOTO BY C.L. CHAN

—

國泰民安
FARMASI / PHARMACY
KK
KOTA KINABALU DISPENSARY SDN. BHD.
30
celcom

政通人和
AGRO
BANK

Above: Who can resist buying a *sompoton*, a local instrument made of bamboo tubes, when it is demonstrated by such charming musicians?
PHOTO BY DAVID KIRKLAND/STB

Perhaps the best place to begin exploring the city is in one of its most attractive areas, the waterfront along the edge of Gaya Bay. Once dominated by a series of makeshift markets, small jetties and even a contractor's storage site, this priceless location with its views across to Pulau Gaya is being transformed.

At its southern end, in front of Promenade Hotel, one can see across a small bay to Sutera Harbour, a development including a resort, housing and recreational activities complete with golf course and marina. Moving northwards towards the city centre, a stretch of the waterfront is currently being privately developed for a hotel and shopping complex, which promises a public boardwalk along the water's edge.

Wooden walkways already built above the sea wall give the various restaurants, bars and other enterprises along the complex known as The Waterfront an enviable location, especially during the cooler evening hours. Locals and visitors alike come here to relax, to have a drink, dine on everything from Malay cuisine to Australian barbecued steak to pub food.

Beyond The Waterfront is a local fruit market (a great place for a drink of refreshing water from young green coconuts), while next to this is the jam-packed collection of small stalls known as the Handicraft Market. This is one of the best places in the city to bargain for souvenirs and handicrafts from Sabah, the Philippines and Indonesia, and is high on the list of places to explore for visitors to Kota Kinabalu.

This page: Kota Kinabalu by night. The balmy night air makes dining at restaurants along The Waterfront an irresistible proposition, with lively bars and nightclubs offering more options late into the night.
PHOTOS BY PEIN LEE/STB

Following pages: The Waterfront, seen from the sea by day, is one of KK's most popular evening spots.
PHOTO BY DAVID KIRKLAND/STB

Past the open-sided markets selling dried fish and fruits (the best place to buy the famed mangoes from the Philippines during the season), the large Central Market (Pasar Am) has a fascinating collection of fresh and dried local produce. You can find just about anything here, from a selection of around a dozen types of rice to yeast for making rice wine; there's everything needed for a betel and areca nut chew to local tobacco; imported grapes and other temperate fruit and even more exciting, if sometimes strange, local tropical fruits. Other sections of the market specialise in poultry and meat, with a separate fish market located right on the water's edge.

Huge gaily painted wooden fishing boats tie up at the edge of one of the market's car parks, while beyond this, the boardwalk of the attractive new Segama Waterfront is a place to sit and enjoy the sea views, to exercise, take souvenir photos, and to smile at the frolicking stone dolphins and the huge marlin leaping from the centre of a traffic roundabout opposite.

Beyond this, past the Marine Police basin, Jesselton Point includes the old jetty of Jesselton, where visiting ships tied up. It is still possible to see train tracks on the jetty, and there's even an old carriage in place, a reminder of the days when produce was taken by rail right to the end of the jetty for loading onto ships. A few enlargements of historic photos strategically placed along Jesselton Point offer a glimpse of this spot in bygone days.

The area has been restored as a departure point for ferries to Labuan, and for boats across to the islands of the Tunku Abdul Rahman Marine Park (these can be booked from inside the air-conditioned terminal building).

Opposite: On the eve of Chinese New Year, the road in front of the Central Market becomes a street market for special festive foods and decorations.
PHOTO BY H.C. CHAN

Above: Fishing boats tie up along the sea wall at the Segama Waterfront.
PHOTO BY H.C. CHAN

Following pages: A traditional welcome for tourists arriving in Kota Kinabalu on a luxurious cruise ship.
PHOTO BY LEE YEN PHIN

CUNARD

Queen Victoria
CUNARD

Previous pages: This leaping marlin near the Segama Waterfront is testament to the trend for decorative statues in the middle of Kota Kinabalu's traffic roundabouts.
PHOTO BY HENRY K.Y. CHIN

—

Above: The edge of the Padang Merdeka is an ideal spot for early morning exercise such as *tai chi* and *chi kung*.
PHOTO BY CHAN SHUK LING

—

Above right: Looking over the city from the Signal Hill Observatory.
PHOTO BY CHAN SHUK LING

—

The original centre of Jesselton was Gaya Street, with the refurbished offices of Sabah Tourism offering an idea of what some of the original buildings once looked like. The city's major banks and legal offices can still be found here and in the parallel Jalan Pantai (Beach Road), which once ran along the shore. The original Chinese provision shops, hardware stores and old-style coffeeshops are fast being replaced by print shops, air-conditioned restaurants, up-market coffeeshops or modern restaurants, pizza places and shops selling mobile phones. Nonetheless, KK Lama (Old Kota Kinabalu) still has traces of the old Jesselton town and is once again one of the busiest parts of town, especially at night.

Every Sunday, Gaya Street is transformed into a 4-block open-air market, a city version of the *tamu*. Extremely popular with both locals and visitors, the market operates from as early as 7 am until noon, with people flocking here to buy orchids, cooked food, fruit trees, clothing, puppies, tropical fish and a host of souvenir items.

Between Gaya Street and the forested hill behind the Jesselton Hotel is an area known to locals as Australia Place, although no road sign bears this name. The road from the Quonset-hut style Multi-purpose Hall and past the old Police Station, a street once almost exclusively occupied by old print shops, rubber stamp makers and stationery shops is now being taken over by backpacker lodges and small private hotels. This area was the camp site for the Australian Forces who helped rebuild

Jesselton after the end of World War II. A corner coffeeshop cum restaurant, the atmospheric Borneo 1945 Museum Kopi Tiam displays wartime photographs of Australian soldiers.

Their efforts are also commemorated in a simple stone memorial at one edge of the tiny City Park, opposite the Central Post Office.

Sitting on the hill just behind Jalan Gaya, the Atkinson Clock Tower is the only downtown pre-war structure to have survived until today. This quaint white-painted rectangular wooden tower, with a clock on just two sides, was built in 1905 in memory of Francis George Atkinson. He was Jesselton's first district officer, and died at only 28 years of age, probably of malaria.

Not far from the Clock Tower and shaded by some magnificent old trees is Jesselton's original sports field, the Padang Merdeka. Home to many important ceremonial events, including the proclamation of the formation on Malaysia on 16 September 1963, the Padang's small size belies its importance in local history.

Signal Hill, so named because it was used to display navigation lights for ships coming in to Jesselton's port, is more correctly known today as Bukit Bendera (though few locals call it that). About two-thirds of the way up the hill, an observatory offers a sweeping view down over the city and across Gaya Bay to the islands which protect Kota Kinabalu from the open waters of the South China Sea.

Above left: The Atkinson Clock Tower, near the Padang Merdeka, is the only structure to have survived World War II completely unscathed.
PHOTO BY C.V. CHONG

Above: The charming Jesselton Hotel, the city's second oldest, in Gaya Street.
PHOTO BY C.L. CHAN

Following pages: The original heart of the city or KK Lama lies between the forest-covered Signal Hill and the sea.
PHOTO BY PEIN LEE/STB

METROJAYA

Above: Night markets held in the street in Segama, Kampung Air and along the waterfront near the Handicraft Market are very popular, even if the occasional rain shower slows business down.

PHOTO BY C.V. CHONG

—

Right: Sabah Tourism Board's office is conveniently located in Gaya Street, near many of the city's hotels, banks, restaurants and shops.

PHOTO BY CHAN SHUK LING

—

Jalan Gaya and the parallel Jalan Pantai house many offices, banks and commercial enterprises, yet the most popular shopping streets are the pedestrian walkways of the Segama district, wedged between the Hyatt Regency Hotel and the Central Post Office. These streets — where you'll find everything from hardware items to cheap clothing, goldsmiths and sellers of barbecued sliced pork — are a great place for people watching.

Even better is the pedestrian bridge that runs from the main road — Jalan Haji Saman — which passes the Post Office. Leading to the Central Market, this wide raised walkway has long been a popular shady spot for sellers of trinkets and handicrafts, who spread their wares on mats on the ground. Most of the vendors are Rungus women, from the northern Kudat region, and some can even be seen wearing traditional dress.

The Sabah State Museum, located near the start of Jalan Penampang, was installed in its current hilltop position in 1965. Its unusual architecture was inspired by the longhouse, the long communal living quarters that were once the standard form of housing for Sabah's indigenous Kadazandusun. The museum offers insights into Sabah's history and ethnography in its galleries, although the unique, outdoor Heritage Village — a series of life-sized recreations of traditional housing for the Rungus, Murut, Kadazan, Bajau, Irranun, Brunei and even early Chinese settlers — is arguably the most interesting section of the entire museum.

Above: An aerial view of the Sabah State Museum.
PHOTO BY PEIN LEE/STB
—
Following pages: The City Mosque, reflected in its surrounding pool, is located at the edge of Likas Bay.
PHOTO BY HENRY K.Y. CHIN
—

Above: Despite its traditional architecture, including a towering pagoda, this complex is not actually a Chinese Temple but the home of a Moral Uplifting Society.
PHOTO BY WENDY HUTTON

Above right: The charming Sikh temple, one of the oldest buildings in Kota Kinabalu, is a mixture of architectural styles.
PHOTO BY WENDY HUTTON

Opposite: The foundation stone for the historic St Michael's Church at Penampang was laid in 1937, but its construction was delayed by WWII.
PHOTO COURTESY OF SABAH TOURISM BOARD

With its multi-ethnic population, Kota Kinabalu is home to a range of places of worship, including mosques, churches, Chinese temples and even a historic Sikh temple. The Sabah State Mosque, located not far from the museum, is a restrained and harmonious building painted a soft grey and embellished with gold. The newer City Mosque, fronted by a pool and facing Likas Bay northeast of the city, is more dramatic in style with its four tall minarets.

The Che Sui Khor Moral Uplifting Society in Jalan Tuaran (the road leading north from Kota Kinabalu) is in traditional Chinese style, with a large traditional pavilion and an 11-storey pagoda vividly decorated with gleaming orange and green tiles.

The staircase leading up to the city's largest Chinese temple, the Poh Toh Tse Buddhist Temple (further along Jalan Tuaran), is flanked by large statues of various deities. Despite its traditional style, the temple is actually relatively new (built in 1980), with a giant statue of the Goddess of Mercy dominating its grounds.

Although there are no Christian churches of any historical or architectural interest, Kota Kinabalu has one of the most idiosyncratic and charming Sikh temples to be found anywhere. Built in 1924 for the small Sikh community, the Gurdwara in Jalan Mat Salleh (on the way to Tanjung Aru) looks almost like an English village church with its stained glass windows set in Gothic arches. The small hexagonal tower (where one almost expects to see a church bell) is topped by a silver dome.

Previous pages: Le Meridien hotel faces the bay, offering a good view of Kota Kinabalu's famed sunsets.
PHOTO BY DAVID KIRKLAND/STB

—

Above: Fishing boats anchored not far from the Sutera Harbour Resort.
PHOTO COURTESY OF LE MERIDIEN K.K.

—

Dried birds' nests, local rice wine (*tapai* or *lihing*), traditional hand-woven textiles and pottery incised with traditional motifs are just some of the unusual items found in Kota Kinabalu's shops and markets. Those who want to spend time shopping can visit open-air night markets, go to a weekly native market or *tamu*, or shop in one of the many air-conditioned shopping complexes found in the city and suburbs.

A perennial favourite, Wisma Merdeka in the heart of the city is typical of what you can expect. A huge range of small enterprises offer optical wear, jewellery, stationery, books, clothing, camera and sound equipment, small department stores, money changers, tailors, hairdressers and shoe shops. You need never go hungry here, with small eateries, international food and coffee franchises and local food courts offering a wide range of food (often at surprisingly low prices). Whatever you're looking for, you'll almost certainly find it here or in the Centrepoint shopping complex (where Palm Square on the 4th floor features more upmarket goods) and the newer Warisan Square.

Perhaps the most upmarket and certainly the newest of the city's shopping complexes, the huge Suria Sabah is located on the waterfront just before the Marine Police depot. A large selection of branded produce can be found in the 4-storey department store, and in the dozens of smaller shops.

Located about 10 minutes from the city, 1 Borneo bills itself as the largest mall in Borneo, with everything from the usual retail shops to a cinema complex. However, its distance from the city limits its appeal to visitors with limited time.

Night markets are still a feature of the city, a left-over from the pre-shopping complex days when locals would buy everything from clothing to toiletries to cooked food from open-air stalls. The night market at Kampung Air, where the stalls are set up each evening around sunset, is a popular spot, while another night market where cooked food predominates is on the waterfront near the Handicraft Market.

Top: The suburban shopping centre, City Mall, one of the city's newest, is particularly popular during the weekends. PHOTO BY C.V. CHONG
Above: The huge complex of 1Borneo, billed as Borneo's largest shopping mall, is north of the city. PHOTO BY LEE YEN PHIN

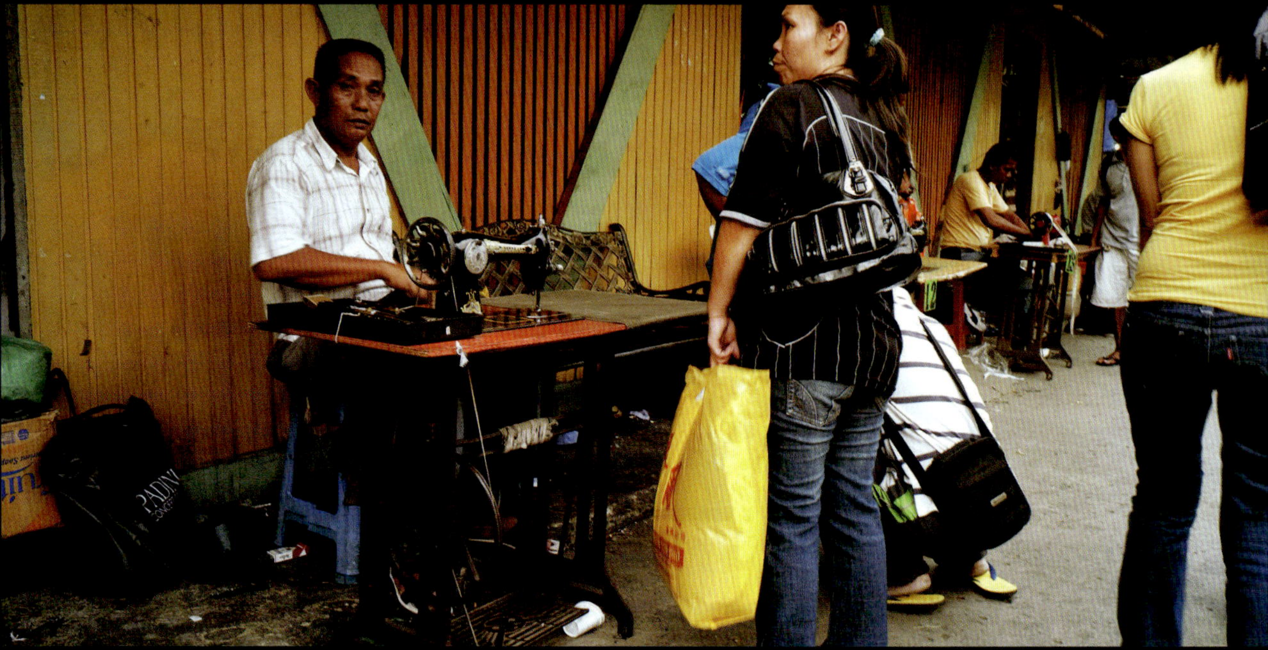

Top: Tailors sit outside the Handicraft Market, ready to handle any sewing task quickly and inexpensively.
Above: Green mangoes, very popular in snacks and salads, arrive at the market. PHOTOS BY PEIN LEE/STB

The bright red ice shaver (top) is a sign that a favourite sweet snack known as ABC is available; various dried fruits, sweet beans and jelly cubes are mixed with shaved ice, evaporated milk and syrup. Ginger and chillies are essential local seasonings. PHOTOS BY PEIN LEE/STB

Fish, both fresh and slathered with chilli and spices before being grilled, are a highlight of this night market set right on the bay. The prices are cheap and the lively atmosphere free. PHOTOS BY PEIN LEE/STB

Every evening, the open space at one side of the Handicraft Market becomes a vibrant Night Market with food as the main attraction. Barbecued fish and chicken wings are two of the most popular offerings. PHOTOS BY PEIN LEE/STB

Above: The smell of freshly ground coffee always draws shoppers to this Gaya Street stall on Sunday mornings.
PHOTO BY PEIN LEE/STB

Another distinctive shopping experience that should not be missed is the Sunday morning open market known as the Gaya Street Fair. From as early as 7 am, the stalls are set up and ready to sell to customers who come first thing to avoid the heat and the crowds that pack the four blocks of Gaya Street as the morning progresses.

Although begun as a market for local handicrafts, the Gaya Street Fair has grown into a bustling bazaar with a huge range of produce. Unusual local vegetables, popular fruits, home-cooked food and freshly ground local coffee tantalise the taste buds, with several open-fronted coffeeshop restaurants along Gaya Street doing a roaring trade in noodles.

Pets and paintings, cacti and kittens, orchids and antiques, handbags and souvenirs, dried medicinal herbs and bottles of wild honey — it's all there and more. Members of The Society for the Blind set up a row of plastic chairs on the pavement and offer foot massage for a remarkably low price, while volunteer nurses will measure your blood pressure.

Still on the subject of health, Kota Kinabalu has seen a large number of spas opening in recent years, most of them located in deluxe hotels or shopping centres. While most of these offer the kind of relaxing massage which can be found in any Asian city, there are a couple of spas specialising in indigenous styles of body therapy, using local herbs and spices.

Left: Foot reflexology carried out by blind masseurs at the Gaya Street Fair each Sunday is so popular that there's invariably a queue of weary shoppers looking for relief.
PHOTO BY CHAN SHUK LING

—

Below left: This stack of small bamboo baskets in a Gaya Street coffeeshop holds delicious steamed titbits known as *dim sum*.
PHOTO BY PEIN LEE/STB

—

Below: The Gaya Street Fair is a good place to shop for handicrafts and souvenirs.
PHOTO BY PEIN LEE/STB

—

Above: An assortment of sea shells from the Philippines.
PHOTO BY C.L. CHAN

—

Above right: Paintings by local artists make a relatively inexpensive souvenir.
PHOTO BY C.L. CHAN

—

Right: Antiques and curios usually include brassware and ceramics.
PHOTO BY PEIN LEE/STB

—

Opposite: The narrow footway between the stalls in Gaya Street is always packed.
PHOTO BY PEIN LEE/STB

—

Following pages: A soaking tub for two in one of the city's many luxurious spas.
PHOTO COURTESY BY SHANGRI-LA'S RASA RIA RESORT

—

Tatoos
&
Bar
UMH

Above: Kota Kinabalu's spas offer both Asian and Western styles of massage and general pampering — an ideal antidote to a busy round of sight-seeing or shopping.
PHOTO BY DAVID KIRKLAND/STB
—

An exfoliating scrub using local coffee and spices after a day in the sun and sea, a firm yet relaxing massage to ease away the aches left after climbing Mount Kinabalu, or a special massage using the thumbs to unblock energy channels and get rid of fatigue are just some of the therapies which can be experienced.

One of the great pleasures of Kota Kinabalu is its wide range of delicious and inexpensive food. Typical multi-racial Malaysian fare (including Chinese, Malay and Indian dishes) is joined by food from around Asia (Japan, Thailand, Indonesia, Vietnam, Korea) as well as Italian, Spanish and other international favourites. Western coffee and food franchises are found in air-conditioned shopping complexes such as Centre Point Sabah, KK Plaza (opposite the Central Market), Warisan Square and Wisma Merdeka.

Malaysian food can be enjoyed in air-conditioned restaurants, with some very good Chinese restaurants found in the suburbs. The widest choice of Malaysian dishes is generally available in the food courts found in most shopping complexes. A wide range of small stalls offer a range of local dishes, displaying the names and prices of each dish. Even if the names don't mean anything to a visitor, it's easy to point to what looks good, or to ask one of the friendly locals what they're eating.

Simple local food can also be enjoyed alfresco during the cooler evening hours; popular spots include the First Beach area of Tanjung Aru Beach and the large complex of stalls and restaurants known as Seri Selera Kampung Air, at the edge of the city centre.

The coffeeshop (know locally as a *kopi tiam*) is a much-loved local institution. These simple shops (although they serve food, "restaurant" is too grand a word) sell hot and cold drinks, and have one or more stalls where specialty dishes are available. There may be a selection of noodles, a range of ready-cooked dishes, a maker of pan-fried pot sticker dumplings or, if it is a Muslim coffeeshop, the flaky griddle-fried bread known as *roti canai*.

Literally "pulled bread", *roti canai* is made from dough which is flung out repeatedly to a tissue-thin circle, folded, then slapped on a griddle to cook until irresistibly crisp and golden. Enjoyed as breakfast or as a substantial snack, the bread is eaten dipped in curry gravy or a thin lentil stew. Coffeeshops in the Segama area of Kota Kinabalu are a good place to find this treat.

Thanks to its tropical climate combined with the nearby cooler foothills of Mount Kinabalu, a huge range of vegetables is grown here — and what doesn't flourish is often imported. Some of the notable local vegetables include fresh wood mushrooms, better known internationally by their Japanese name, *shiitake*; a slender crisp stem with small bright green leaves called Sabah vegetable or *sayur manis*; wild fern tips which are excellent stir-fried with dried prawns or a spicy *sambal*.

Above: Coffee shops or open-fronted casual restaurants, found in suburban shopping areas as well as in the city, offer some of the best and least expensive food around.
PHOTO COURTESY OF SABAH TOURISM BOARD

Above: Vivid pink dragon fruit, originally from Central America, are now widely grown in Sabah. The red-fleshed durian, encased in a thorny golden shell (seen to the right) is, however, endemic to Borneo.

PHOTO BY CHAN SHUK LING

—

Right: Not surprisingly given their shape, these golden fruit are known as starfruit; they have a slightly astringent juice, making them very refreshing at the end of a meal.

PHOTO BY H.C. CHAN

—

Far right: Grown on a very thorny jungle palm, the skin of this fruit gives it the descriptive name of snake fruit or *salak*.

PHOTO BY C.V. CHONG

—

Exploring the City

All the well-known tropical fruits can be found in Kota Kinabalu, plus a few less common ones including the aptly named star fruit, crisp and slightly acidic; notoriously pungent durian with its spiky exterior and meltingly smooth butter-coloured flesh; various types of wood apple or *jambu* and sweet round white *rambutan* which nestle inside a hairy red skin. One unusual way of eating certain fruits here is to dip them in a brownish-red powder made from ground dried plums, which adds a wonderful sweet-sour accent.

The usual meats and poultry are found here, although Muslim restaurants and most hotel restaurants do not serve pork. Venison from deer raised in Sabah is sometimes found in Chinese restaurants.

Almost all visitors to Kota Kinabalu have heard of its magnificent seafood, and at least one meal in a popular seafood restaurant is a must. For most visitors, the prices of seafood here are very much cheaper than at home, while the selection is little short of amazing.

Some of the most popular seafood restaurants are along the city's waterfront area, as well as in the Sri Selera complex of Kampung Air and near Tanjung Aru. Rather than ordering from a menu, most diners look at the range of fresh and live seafood, choose what they want, and then discuss with the restaurant staff how they would like it cooked. As well as choice fish, there are live prawns, mantis shrimps, lobsters, many different types of shells and crabs. An array of fresh green vegetables, beancurd dishes and fresh fruits promises a true feast.

Below left: Clams are just one of the many varieties of edible shells found in seafood restaurants.

—

Below right: No seafood meal is complete without succulent, meaty mud crabs, caught in the coastal mangrove areas.

—

PHOTOS BY DANIEL WONG

5.
Islands in the Sun

Lazing on the sandy beach which slides gently into the jade-turquoise sea, you gaze from your "treasure island" towards the undulating dark green hills, stretching into infinity. They embody the mystery and magic of Borneo, ageless and seemingly untouched. But as your eye travels slowly north, buildings begin to create silhouettes against the wall of green: a resort or two, a marina, a golf course, then gleaming high-rise buildings.

It seems almost impossible that you could be so close to the city while enjoying the peace and beauty of a tropical isle, or strolling upon a long, almost-deserted beach just minutes from downtown. Yet this is the reality of Sabah's west coast, blessed with a series of fine sandy beaches from far south in Brunei Bay up along the edge of the Klias Peninsula; on through Kimanis and Papar to Kota Kinbalu's much-loved Tanjung Aru beach. North of the city, the beaches continue through Karambunai, Tuaran and along the coast west of Kota Belud.

As if this abundance of beaches were not enough, there is also a string of picture-postcard islands. From Pulau Tiga off the Klias Peninsula on up to the islands of Gaya Bay and on northwards to Mantanani in Kota Belud district, each island holds its special charm.

Opposite: This marina, where local and visiting boats find safe harbour, is also a departure point for boat trips to the islands of Tunku Abdul Rahman Marine Park, around 15 minutes away.
PHOTO BY PEIN LEE/STB

—

Following pages: A steady stream of speedboats deliver visitors to Pulau Sapi, seen to the left and separated from Pulau Gaya by a very narrow channel.
PHOTO BY ROGER MUNNS/SCUBAZOO

—

Kota Kinabalu

Tunku Abdul Rahman Marine Park consists of:

1. Pulau Gaya
2. Pulau Sapi
3. Pulau Manukan
4. Pulau Sulug
5. Pulau Mamutik

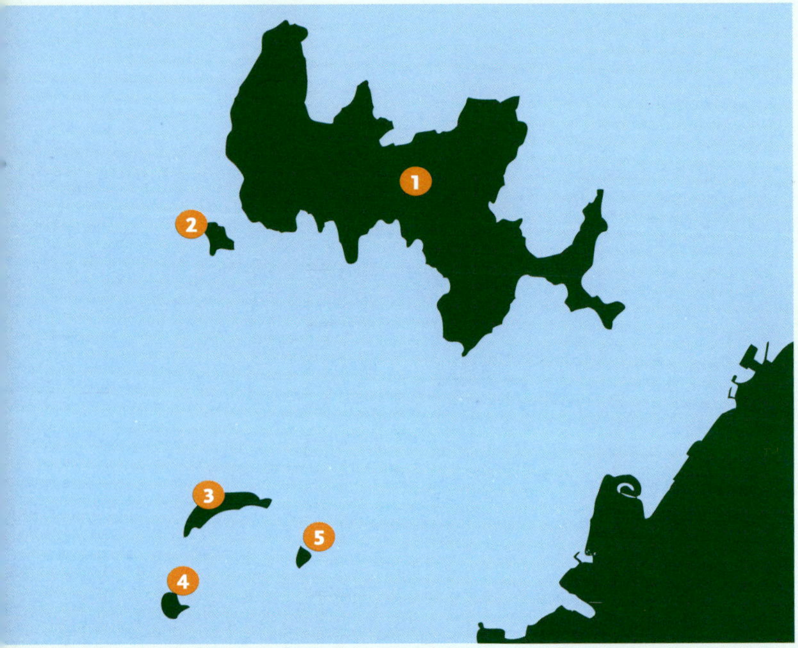

Opposite: The jetty at Pulau Sapi, the most popular of the islands in the Tunku Abdul Rahman Marine Park, leads onto a fine white sandy beach.
PHOTO BY H.C. CHAN

—

Following pages: The view from infinity-edge swimming pool at the Gayana Resort, on the edge of the Sabah Park's reserve on Pulau Gaya, makes this spot seem very far away from Sabah's bustling capital.
PHOTO BY DAVID KIRKLAND/STB

—

A hilly island — so close you feel could almost reach across the water and touch it — is the main reason for Kota Kinabalu's location. Sitting directly across from today's city, Pulau Gaya is the largest of several islands sheltering Gaya Bay from the open sea, making the area behind it, in the words of a 19th-century colonial, an "admirable harbour".

When the Chartered Company decided to establish a west coast settlement in 1882, they selected Gaya, then home to a few Bajau fishermen who referred to the island as *gayoh* or big (leading to the name Gaya). However, a rebellious Bajau by the name of Mat Salleh burned the Gaya settlement to the ground, forcing the relocation of the settlement on the nearby coast.

Gaya today is the largest of the five islands making up the Tunku Abdul Rahman Park, one of Kota Kinabalu's greatest treasures. The marine park was created in 1974 to preserve the flora and fauna of the islands and their surrounding waters. Although a small part of Gaya is occupied by several villages — most of them building over shallow waters outside the Park boundaries — the rest of the island has steep forested hills and ravines, with a few small streams. The forest crowds right down to a series of bays, with an interesting patch of mangrove forest near Camp Bay on the southwest side of the Park, and another in Malohom Bay.

The lowland rainforest on islands always has fewer species of plants and animals than on the mainland, yet is still very rewarding. One of the most dramatic birds that can be seen on Gaya is the Asian Pied Hornbill, a huge black and white bird with a massive yellow and white casque. Sea eagles, too, hover on high or make their nests on some of the tallest trees within the forest. Below, squirrels, wild pigs, dragon-like monitor lizards and wild boar can sometimes be spotted. Macaques, self-confident monkeys that seem to have no fear of humans, can be found on Gaya though seem to prefer Sapi, attracted by the rich pickings left by visitors.

Although most visitors to Pulau Gaya come to enjoy its beaches, a stroll along one of the trails will provide a glimpse of the forest and some of its inhabitants. It is possible to take a trail from beyond Camp Bay's jetty, then taking the boardwalk over the mangrove swamp where crabs and mudskipper fish can be seen and kingfishers often sit waiting for a tasty morsel. The trail then climbs up through the forested hills and descends at Padang Point.

100
100

Above: The polyps of a sea fan look like delicate white flowers.
PHOTO BY GIL WOOLLEY/SCUBAZOO
—
Far left: Patient divers with sharp eyes could well spot a juvenile broadclub cuttlefish (*Sepia latimanus*).
PHOTO BY GIL WOOLLEY/SCUBAZOO
—
Left: Despite its beauty, this lion fish is venomous.
PHOTO BY GIL WOOLLEY/SCUBAZOO
—
Opposite: A shoal of tiny reef fish swim over corals, including pink and white soft coral.
PHOTO BY SEOK WUN AU YONG/ SCUBAZOO
—
Following pages: A huge jelly fish, attended by a shoal of fish.
PHOTO BY SEOK WUN AU YONG/ SCUBAZOO
—

Opposite: The piling of a jetty attracts a range of marine life.
PHOTO BY SEOK WUN AU YONG/ SCUBAZOO

—

Above: A tiny red hairy crab rests on a bed of polyps.
PHOTO BY GIL WOOLLEY/SCUBAZOO

—

Left: This blue-ringed octopus, seen in the waters of Tunku Abdul Rahman Marine Park, is venomous.
PHOTO BY JASON ISLEY/SCUBAZOO

—

Following pages: An anemone fish (popularly known as Nemo after a movie cartoon character) seeks protection among the stinging tentacles of a sea anemone.
PHOTO BY JASON ISLEY/SCUBAZOO

—

Above: A long jetty leads to the beach at Padang Point, a beach on Pulau Gaya opposite Pulau Sapi.
PHOTO BY H.C. CHAN

Separated from Gaya by a narrow, shallow channel, Pulau Sapi is small by comparison, basically a forested ridge with sandy fringes on one side and a rocky shore facing the open sea. A jetty, safe swimming beaches, picnic tables and other facilities plus the availability of water sports equipment (including "sea walking" under water with a special helmet with breathing apparatus) make Sapi a favourite among visitors, especially tour groups. Yet despite the numbers of visitors, it is still possible to see a turtle surfacing for air just off the beach, or to watch a hornbill flap-flap-glide, flap-glap-glide overhead.

The most developed island within the Park, Pulau Manukan is long and narrow, with a relatively low ridge of hills separating the developed side of the island from its rocky, ocean-facing side. Chalets offers accommodation to those who find the idea of a night on the island irresistible. There's a restaurant, although some visitors prefer to enjoy a barbecue prepared by their tour company, or take a packed picnic lunch.

Water sports operators on Manukan offer everything from snorkelling to scuba diving, and visitors can even rent an underwater scooter with special breathing apparatus. A trail leaving from the coast on the developed side of the island climbs up along the ridge, offering views down to the rocky shore and out over the ocean.

Above: Non-divers can don special apparatus and walk on the sea floor off Pulau Gaya to see underwater life face to face.

PHOTO BY MATT OLDFIELD/SCUBAZOO

Just one-quarter the size of Manukan, Pulau Mamutik is a delightful little isle with two beaches, some very attractive corals, the usual picnic, barbecue and toilet facilities, a small café and a scuba diving operation based in what was a private home before the island became part of the Park.

The furthest of the islands from Kota Kinabalu, Pulau Sulug offers unadorned nature and the best scuba diving in the Park off its southwest corner. The total lack of tourism facilities makes Sulug appealing to only a few visitors, who revel in the simplicity of its long sand spit and forested hill and are happy to forgo the convenience of a jetty for peace and privacy.

Dinawan, a low, largely rocky island off the coastal village of Kinarut, has an attractive shallow lagoon but does not offer the kind of beaches most visitors come in search of. Further south, however, Pulau Tiga has something to fulfil almost every dream. How about mud volcanoes where warm, mineral-rich mud burps up through the ground? Beaches where yours are the only footprints?

You'll also find the megapode, a bird that lets the sun and sand incubate its eggs; huge monitor lizards resembling miniature dragons; golden beaches lapped by the warm sea; orchids blooming in massive shade trees, perky Magpie Robins and Dollar Birds with their distinctive pale under-wing patches.

Above: Bathing in the soft warm mud volcano pools is an essential (and often hilarious) rite for visitors to Pulau Tiga.
PHOTO BY SCUBAZOO

—

Opposite. This small rocky island is an important breeding ground for sea snakes, hence its name, Snake Island.
PHOTO BY JASON ISLEY/SCUBAZOO

—

Pulau Tiga — 10 km off the coast and reached via Kuala Penyu — is Sabah's youngest island, created in 1897 by a large-scale eruption from the mud volcanoes which still burble gently near the island's northern shores. Glorious unspoiled lowland rainforest covers the 158-square-kilometre island, protected as a forest reserve since 1933. In 1978, Tiga and two islands just north of it — Kalampunian Damit (eroded to a mere wisp of blinding white sand) and rocky Kalampunian Besar (an important breeding ground for sea snakes) — were gazetted as the Pulau Tiga Marine Park, administered by Sabah Parks.

On the south side of the island, next to Sabah Park's ranger station, the comfortable and ideally located Pulau Tiga Resort offers visitors a place to enjoy the barefoot-on-the-beach life. A more basic resort set on the isolated east side of the island, Borneo Survivor Resort is a reminder of Pulau Tiga's nickname, "Survivor Island". An American reality TV show was filmed here, the participants dropped on a northern beach and left to survive virtually unaided during the course of the filming. Little did they know that Sabah Park's base and the Pulau Tiga Resort were on the other side of the island.

There are several trails through the Tiga's forest, the most popular leading to the mud volcano area and on to a couple of beaches. Shallow pools have been scooped out to allow the flowing mud to accumulate, making a popular place for children and adults alike to frolic like water buffaloes in the soft silky mud.

Another interesting group of three islands lies north of Sabah, about an hour by speedboat off Rampayan in the Kota Belud district, or reached via Ambong Bay west of Kota Belud. The main island, Mantanani Besar, is settled by a number of fishing families, while almost joined to its southern tip is a tiny rocky isle, Lingisan; further south is the third island, the uninhabited Mantanani Kecil or "Little Mantanani".

The Mantanani islands are protected as a bird sanctuary for two species of tropical frigatebird, superb oceanic gliders which soar effortlessly on thermals. These huge black "pirates of the sky", with their distinctive forked tails, dive with incredible speed to force other birds to drop their catch, which they then steal and eat. Both the Lesser Frigatebird and the endangered Christmas Island Frigatebird, which flies to this Indian Ocean island to breed, create an amazing spectacle every dusk as they fly in to roost on trees on the slopes of Lingisan. They cannot take off from the ground nor from the surface of the sea, and need the height of these trees to get airborne each morning.

A type of sea grass grows on the shallow sea floor off certain areas of Mantanani. This is the food of the endangered dugong or "sea cow", a 200–300 kg mammal which suckles its young. Dugongs have been seen off Mantanani's southern beach, sometimes remaining in the vicinity for several months. They have even been known to swim fearlessly among scuba divers. Even without the dugongs, Mantanani offers some of the best diving off Sabah's west coast, with relatively shallow coral reefs offering a variety of marine life, including beautiful nudibranchs, basically colourful sea snails without shells.

There is a resort on the main island, although it opens only when there are bookings. A diving operator maintains a picnic area with toilet facilities on the idyllic sandy peninsula on the north of Mantanani, offering day trips from Kota Kinabalu. To the south, uninhabited Mantanani Kecil has a simple dive lodge built on stilts over the sea, well sheltered from the southwest winds which blow from about May to November.

Opposite: The simple dive lodge at Mantanani Kecil offers divers a place to stay.
PHOTO BY ROGER MUNNS/SCUBAZOO

Above left: A long white sandy beach on the north of the main island of Mantanani is a great picnic spot.
PHOTO BY GIL WOOLLEY/SCUBAZOO

Above right: A diver explores the entrance of an underwater cave on Mantanani.
PHOTO BY JASON ISLEY/SCUBAZOO

Following pages: Pulau Sapi in the foreground, with Manukan directly behind and Mamutik to the centre left, lie close to the coastline of Kota Kinabalu, backed by the Crocker Range.
PHOTO BY LEE YEN PHIN

Top left: Shady trees and small shelters are found at the edge of Tanjung Aru Beach.
PHOTO BY H.C. CHAN

—

Above: A colony of resident parakeets can be seen and heard in the casuarina trees lining the beach.
PHOTO BY WENDY HUTTON

—

Above right: The ideally located Shangri-La's Tanjung Aru Resort was the first 5-star hotel in Sabah.
PHOTO BY LEE YEN PHIN

—

The best-loved beach in all of Sabah is Tanjung Aru Beach, stretching 2 km from the edge of Kota Kinabalu International Airport up to a small peninsula occupied by a 5-star resort. For most of its length, the beach is backed by parkland or grassy areas dotted with coconut palms or casuarina trees, making ideal camping or picnic spots.

Just 6 km from the city and easily reached by bus, Tanjung Aru Beach attracts locals from all walks of life. It is the city's favourite "green lung", soothing and relaxing the mind and body with the gentle ebb and flow of the sea and the faint sound of the wind sighing through the huge *aru* or casuarina trees which give the beach its name.

In the early morning, groups of older folk practise *tai chi* while the more energetic jog past beach cleaners raking the sand. When the tide is very low and the shallow reef near the resort end of the beach is exposed, people poke around looking for edible shells or simply discovering the wonders of the reef.

There are plenty of places for a snack or meal along Tanjung Aru Beach. The area known as First Beach has a café and couple of restaurants, with a covered food centre adjacent. All kinds of inexpensive meals, local tit-bits, fresh tropical fruit and drinks can be enjoyed here.

—

PHOTOS BY CHAN SHUK LING

By late afternoon, the next round of joggers is joined by strolling lovers, children making sandcastles or splashing in the sea, a bunch of young men playing football and keen photographers with their cameras poised on tripods hoping for one of the most spectacular sunsets in the world. The sun drops quickly here just north of the equator, the fiery red ball sinking rapidly into the South China Sea. The play of red, orange, purple, duck-egg blue and indigo that lights up the sky after the sun has set compensates for the short time it is on display with a spectacular intensity.

Although it is one continuous strip of sand, locals have always referred to separate beaches along Tanjung Aru. Thus, the area near the Kinabalu Golf Club and Kinabalu Yacht Club has always been known as First Beach, and is the focal point for many visitors. For years, First Beach was home to clusters of simple food stalls selling favourite local snacks such as boiled sweetcorn, pickled fruits, steamed peanuts and seasonal fruits (particularly durians), as well as popular drinks such as young green coconut water or freshly pressed sugar cane juice.

Relatively recently, the facilities of First Beach were rebuilt and most of the old food stalls relocated in a roofed food centre, Anjung Perdana, maintained by the City Council. Next to this, the privately managed First Beach Complex consists of a couple of restaurants, a coffee bar and a café-cum-bar with tables set out on a boardwalk right above the beach.

Further down towards the airport, another cluster of original, old-style food stalls selling Muslim food still remains at Second Beach, just beyond Prince Philip Park.

While Tanjung Aru Beach offers a number of facilities, other beaches beyond the city remain much the same as they have for generations, their lack of facilities and often deserted status making them rare treasures in today's crowded world.

Visit, for example, the coast near Kampung Shabandar in Tuaran district, or the stretch of coastline running from Kuala Penyu on up beyond Binsuluk. You could be

Opposite: The beach at sunset is popular with young and old.
PHOTO BY HENRY K.Y. CHIN

—

Above left: During the northeast monsoon, the beach of Tanjung Aru is generally sheltered from the prevailing wind and makes an attractive anchorage for visiting cruising yachts.
PHOTO BY C.V. CHONG

—

Above: Tanjung Aru beach at sunset is an ideal spot to walk the family dog.
PHOTO BY HENRY K.Y. CHIN

—

Following pages: It's hard to think of anywhere better placed for relaxation than the Chi spa, on its own tiny islet at Shangri-La's Tanjung Aru Resort.
PHOTO COURTESY BY SHANGRI-LA'S RASA RIA RESORT

—

Above: An old fibreglass boat used for fishing just off the beach.
PHOTO BY H.C. CHAN

—

Above right: A small crab scuttles between the sand balls made by burrowing crabs along the beach.
PHOTO BY C.V. CHONG

—

Opposite: Optimist yachts line up in front of the Kinabalu Yacht Club, where races are held every Sunday.
PHOTO BY HENRY K.Y. CHIN

—

Following pages: The Sampan Bar at Shangri-La's Rasa Ria Resort in Tuaran, north of Kota Kinabalu, offers peace and seclusion, ideal for sunset musings.
PHOTO COURTESY BY SHANGRI-LA'S RASA RIA RESORT

—

the only person in sight unless a few fishermen are about to launch their simple canoes, or a herd of water buffaloes lumber by in search of something to graze on. If you're lucky and visit the beach by night, you may even encounter a sea turtle coming to lay her eggs after digging a hole in the sand.

Along these sandy shores are specially adapted trees and shrubs, many of them grown from seeds which have washed up with the tide. In some areas, flowering creepers add a splash of colour on the sand. If you spend an entire day by the beach, you may be able to watch the Sea Hibiscus, a bright yellow flower in the morning, slowly fading to a reddish brown.

Another distinctive plant found near the beach on islands, as well as the mainland, is the Seashore Screwpine (*Pandanus odoratissimus*), a branching tree with spiky green fronds and pineapple-like fruits which turn orangey-red when ripe.

The *Barringtonia asiatica* or Fish Poison Tree has exquisite scented flowers which open at dusk, long silky filaments of bright pink bleaching to silvery white, with yellow dots at the tip or each. These beautiful big flowers can often be seen lying on the sand the following day, while the seed pods, like a large wooden square or a boxy coconut, can float for miles on the ocean to sprout on some far-flung foreign shore.

Unlike beaches in many other areas, there is not an abundance of shells along Sabah's west coast, although sometimes one encounters literally thousands of the same species washed in with the tide. Trails of round balls of damp sand the size of a pin head mark the presence of a tiny burrowing crab near the tide line. The traces of certain burrowing shells are quickly recognised by locals, who sometimes come with special rakes to gather the bounty of the sea.

MAS
1022
LSS 11

6. Sabah's Crowning Glory

The mountains of the Crocker Range slash through the centre of Sabah, running from north to south like the jagged spine of a huge green dragon. Behind Kota Kinabalu, the dragon rears its head, creating the magnificent mountain after which the city is named.

Although Mount Kinabalu is the crowning glory of Sabah, the remainder of Crocker Range also offers an remarkable diversity of plant life and wildlife. To protect this natural heritage — some of it found nowhere else in the world — two parks have been created: Kinabalu Park and Crocker Range National Park.

The richness and diversity of Mount Kinabalu and its surroundings are so exceptional that Kinabalu Park was declared Malaysia's first UNESCO World Heritage Site in 2000.

Covering some 754 square kilometres, Kinabalu Park is not only home to rare plants, birds and insects but is an exciting adventure destination offering the challenge of climbing one of Southeast Asia's highest peaks. It is also a place to unwind in spring-like temperatures, or to relax in therapeutic hot springs in the Park's eastern lowlands.

Visible from afar (when weather conditions permit), Kinabalu has always dominated the landscape and mythology of Sabah's indigenous people. For them, *Aki Nabalu* or the Solitary Ancestor is a place of legends, and the sacred resting place of departed souls. At 4,093 metres and still growing a few millimetres each year, Mount Kinabalu is the youngest non-volcanic mountain in the world. It is almost twice the height of the surrounding mountains, its jagged granite core bursting upwards through the green-clad slopes of the Crocker Range to give the mountain a fierce majesty quite unlike any other mountain in the world.

Opposite: A few clumps of tenacious plants cling to the granite slopes of Mount Kinabalu's summit plateau. Orchids can be found as high as 3,300 metres.
PHOTO BY C.V. CHONG

—

Following pages: The distinctive silhouette of Mount Kinabalu, seen from Telipok hills just northeast of the city.
PHOTO BY LOI PUI KING

—

Above: Climbers are often literally above the clouds as they reach the higher levels on Mount Kinabalu, where they are rewarded with breathtaking views. PHOTOS BY CLARENCE CHIANG

Sabah's Crowning Glory

The gateway to Kinabalu Park, Park Headquarters near Kundasang, is only 90 kilometres from Kota Kinabalu, yet given the steep winding road that leads there — not to mention the countless temptations to stop en route — the journey normally takes at least 1 1/2 hours.

Sabah Parks maintains a number of ranger stations apart from Park Headquarters, which is located roughly 1,500 metres above sea level on the southern slopes of the mountain. Some 40 kilometres by road from Headquarters, Poring (550 metres) is a region of hot springs and typical lowland forest, while high on the eastern slopes of the mountain, Mesilau (at almost 2,000 metres) offers yet another perspective of this remarkable Park.

On the western side of Kinabalu Park, accessible via the town of Kota Belud, the sub-station of Sayat Sayat is located beside a scenic river and small waterfall, while on the Park's far northern boundary, Serinsim (reached via Kota Marudu) sits between two sparkling clean rivers and is a favourite camping and picnicking spot.

Kinabalu Park Headquarters offers a wide range of facilities for visitors including a couple of restaurants, accommodation (from hostels to large, fully equipped chalets), nature trails, guided walks, the Kinabalu Natural History Gallery, Mount Kinabalu Botanical Garden and the operation centre for climbers heading for the summit. And high up near the summit plateau, climbers with a head for heights can experience the world's highest *via ferrata*, a system of cables, bridges and ropes that lets them explore the rockface in safety.

Above left: The Panar Laban Resthouse, where most climbers spend the night, rising before dawn the following day to make the final ascent to the summit.
PHOTO BY CLARENCE CHIANG

Above: Weary climbers descending towards the Resthouse and a well-earned breakfast.
PHOTO BY CLARENCE CHIANG

Following pages: Mist along the summit trail gives an ethereal beauty to the forest.
PHOTO BY C.V. CHONG

Climbers often travel up to Park Headquarters in the morning and spend the rest of the day exploring the area. After a night's rest, they leave for Timpohon Gate to begin the climb up to Panar Laban Rata, 4–5 hours away and located at around 3,350 metres. A rest house and hostel offer food and accommodation for the evening, with climbers usually getting up well before dawn to climb for another 2 hours to Low's Peak. With any luck, they will be rewarded with a spectacular sunrise and be able to see the northern tip of Borneo, as well as down over the lower mountains and across the coastal plains to the waters of the South China Sea.

Above: The glossy young leaves of *Vaccinium* sp. found at 3,800 m on Mount Kinabalu. About 40 species of *Vaccinium*, a relative of the Blueberry family, are found in Borneo; the genus is represented by 14 (nearly one-third of the total) on Kinabalu.
PHOTO BY ROBERT NEW

The trail up to the summit plateau offers an insight into the variety of ecosystems within the Park, passing from the lower montane rainforest around Park Headquarters through different types of vegetation, including the atmospheric mossy region or cloud forest, where wisps of moss and lichen hang from the trees and mist often swirls up the valleys. As the trail leads higher, the trees and shrubs of the sub-alpine forest are stunted, and unlikely plants such as wild raspberries can be found. Once the granite slabs of the summit plateau are reached, even the last tenuous plants and orchids clinging to pockets of soil between the rocks are no longer seen. Only the unadorned majesty of the mountain remains.

The exceptional diversity found within Kinabalu Park is due to differences in altitude, climate, soil and geology. One botanist who spent many years studying the Park's plant life aptly described it as "the richest and most remarkable assemblage of plants in the world".

This wondrous biodiversity was unknown to the outside world until the first Western explorers set their sights on conquering the summit. Sir Hugh Low, who worked for the British colonial administration on the island of Labuan, off southwestern Sabah, made the first attempt in 1851. The initial challenge was to reach the base of the mountain; Low and his party of porters and guides had to travel from the coast, across the Tempasuk plain and then upwards through densely forested foothills before they came to the lower slopes of Kinabalu.

Low eventually reached the summit plateau, but failed to find and scale the highest peak, not surprisingly as there are seven peaks over 3,900 metres high. Low made a second attempt in 1858, but although Spenser St John, who accompanied him, scaled South Peak (3,933 metres), once again, the party failed to locate and climb the highest peak. It was only in 1887 that John Whitehead, an English zoologist after whom several species of endemic birds are named, climbed the true summit, naming it, in a most gentlemanly fashion, Low's Peak.

Above left: The twisted trunks of trees growing at sub-alpine level are the result of exposure to strong winds.

PHOTO BY CLARENCE CHIANG

—

Above: The pretty white flowers of *Schima*, and red bell-like flowers of Heath Rhododendron are characteristic of the vegetation around Laban Rata.

PHOTO BY CLARENCE CHIANG

—

Left: The thrusting granite peaks on the summit plateau resemble petrified flames.

PHOTO BY ROBERT NEW

—

Following pages: A guide rope snakes across the granite slabs near the summit, where jagged peaks look like petrified flames.

PHOTO BY C.V. CHONG

—

Although Low and St John collected a number of botanical specimens (including the giant *Nepenthes rajah* pitcher plant), it was botanists and plant collectors like Thomas Lobb, F.W. Burbidge and Miss Lillian Gibbs, a botanist from the British Museum (Natural History), who helped spread awareness of the treasures growing on the slopes of Mount Kinabalu.

Varying geology — such as exposed ridges, peat forests or river valleys — at the same altitude produces different micro-climates and therefore different species. Not surprisingly, given its range of altitudes and micro-climates, Kinabalu Park is home to at least 800 species of orchid. Rare and exquisitely beautiful slipper orchids such as *Paphiopedilum rothschildianum* (an endemic found only in Kinabalu Park and Crocker Range) and *P. lowii* are just a couple of these often spectacular orchids.

Necklaces of orchids hanging down from trees (such as *Coelogyne rhabdobulbon*), translucent white blooms sparkling like stars in the dark forest, improbably coloured green orchids with black markings and the cinnamon-scented, rat-tail orchid (*Paraphalaenopsis labukensis*) are among the countless gloriously beautiful orchids that grow within the Park. Orchid lovers will find a collection of species gathered within the Mount Kinabalu Botanical Garden at Park Headquarters, and an even better collection in the landscaped gardens of the Poring Orchid Conservation Centre.

Opposite: A rare slipper orchid (*Paphiopedilum rothschildianum*) grows wild nowhere in the world apart from the Crocker Range, including Kinabalu Park.
PHOTO BY ANTHONY LAMB

Above left: Another rare orchid, *Paraphalaenopsis labukensis*, which smells of cinnamon.
PHOTO BY ANTHONY LAMB

Above: Cascading sprays of the lovely Necklace Orchid (*Coelogyne radioferens*).
PHOTO BY RICH ELLIS

Above: One of the most common yet beautiful rhododendrons in Kinabalu Park is *Rhododendron lowii*.
PHOTO BY ANTHONY LAMB

—

Right: This rhododendron (*Rhododendron kinabaluensis*) is found only in Kinabalu Park and the higher mountains of the Crocker Range.
PHOTO BY ANTHONY LAMB

—

Opposite: Fat pitchers of the *Nepenthes rajah*, a pitcher plant found only on Mount Kinabalu and neighbouring Mount Tambuyukon. It can be seen growing above the Mesilau River in the eastern side of Kinabalu Park.
PHOTO BY CH'IEN LEE

—

Pitcher plants or *Nepenthes* are another botanical treasure found in Kinabalu Park. Pitcher plants have evolved to live on poor soils, taking their nutrition from insects which are attracted to the sap inside their pitcher. Unable to escape back up the slippery walls, the insects are drowned then dissolved by the enzymes within the pitcher's fluid.

Some of the Park's pitcher plants can be seen at the Mount Kinabalu Botanical Garden at Park Headquarters, although the most spectacular collection is at Mesilau. Here, the giant *Nepenthes rajah* (which can hold up to 1 litre of water) has been transplanted to a hillside garden. Two other species naturally found around Mesilau, *N. fusca* (which has a dark wine-red neck) and *N. tentaculata* (with hairs on the top of its lid) also cling to the same steep slope. In addition, *N. burbidgeae* with its lovely funnel-shaped pitchers blotched with pink has been transplanted here.

Showy rhododendrons with sunshine yellow, pale orange, waxy white or scarlet flowers are also found in the Park, with some 28 different species recorded, several of them endemic. Flowering rhododendrons can often be seen alongside the main summit trail, beginning at Timpohon Gate beyond Park Headquarters, and also near the Nature Centre at Mesilau.

Above: The strange fleshy bloom of the Rafflesia — the world's largest flower — blooms near Kinabalu Park and on the Crocker Range.
PHOTO BY C.L. CHAN

One of the most dramatic flowers found within the Park and its surroundings is the massive Rafflesia, named after Singapore's founder, Sir Stamford Raffles, who first came across the plant in Sumatra. This strange parasitic bloom takes months to mature, and when it opens, measures between 50 cm to 1 metre in diameter. Private owners of sites just outside the Park borders put signs by the road when a Rafflesia is in bloom, particularly several villages on the road to Poring, and also just beyond Poring itself. (Another reserve dedicated to the preservation of the Rafflesia is located on the edge of Crocker Range Park.)

The trails around Park Headquarters wind through the forest along tumbling streams, up forested hills and along narrow ridges. The sharp-eyed visitor will spot insects including butterflies, squirrels and birds as well as the varied trees, shrubs and creepers. When it comes to birds, Kinabalu Park offers "many local curiosities and specialties" including species found only in mountainous regions, including 58 strictly montane birds, 17 of which are endemic Bornean species.

While the Park's trails and the Mount Kinabalu Botanical Garden offer the chance of catching sight of some of these birds, an even better option is to watch at the roadsides in the early morning, when birds are attracted to insects that have congregated near the street lights.

Many of the Park's botanical riches have been gathered together in an area conveniently close to the main Park buildings. Known as the Mount Kinabalu Botanical Garden, this has an easy cemented trail winding through virgin forest, with a number of plants transferred here for easy viewing. This garden can also be a good spot for catching sight of some of Kinabalu's birds, especially in small clearings.

En route for Mesilau, the highest ranger station within Kinabalu Park, the road passes through the vegetable growing area of Kundasang. A long line of stalls selling locally grown vegetables and flowers clusters along the main road to Sandakan, near the side road leading to Mesilau. Just down this road, a fortress-like stone structure can be seen on the hillside on the right: the Kundasang War Memorial. Established in 1962, this commemorates the Australian and British Prisoners of War who died in Sandakan and during the infamous death marches to Ranau during World War II. The memorial also remembers the brave people of North Borneo, who risked their lives to help the POWs.

It is well worth visiting the Memorial for its carefully tended gardens: the Australian Garden, the English Garden with its roses, the Borneo Garden with some magnificent slipper orchids and other mountain rarities, and the tranquil Contemplation Garden and Pool. At the edge of this, there is a view over the crowded farms below and, on a clear day, the sight of the southeastern side of Mount Kinabalu.

Above left: The Kundasang War Memorial commemorates the Allied prisoners- of-war who lost their lives during the Japanese occupation, and the Borneo people who helped them whenever possible.

—

Above: Looking down on the Australian Garden, where the shape of Australia is marked with stones in the centre of the lawn.

—

PHOTOS BY C.V. CHONG

Below: As the Summit Trail reaches the 5 km mark, the vegetation becomes more sparse and stunted.
PHOTO BY ASRAR MAKRANI

Situated at almost 2,000 metres on the eastern flanks of the mountain, Mesilau is wetter, wilder and strikingly different to Park Headquarters. This more remote part of the Park attracts fewer visitors, although not for lack of facilities; the Mesilau Nature Resort (opened in 1998) offers a cluster of accommodation nestled in the forest, and an attractive restaurant built over a fast-flowing forest stream.

The weather at Mesilau can change quite dramatically, with clouds often descending by mid-morning. Unless visitors stay overnight and wander the main road near the restaurant or Nature Centre in the early morning, they are unlikely to see the stunning ring of jagged peaks crowning Mount Kinabalu.

When there is heavy rain on the summit, the water races down the granite slopes and pours into rivers which rage down the valleys. At times like this, the river running below Mesilau's chalets fills with water at an astonishing rate. The often misty afternoons are fresh, to say the least, while at night, the temperatures often drop to around 10–15°C.

Sabah Parks maintains an interesting Nature Centre at Mesilau, where photographs and information panels on some of flora and fauna of Kinabalu Park are displayed. From here, visitors can arrange to take a guided 20-minute trail walk to the hillside Nepenthes Garden, and with luck, view some wild orchids on the way.

Another trail leads through a world of dense vegetation in a loop behind the restaurant. Because of the low light and thick plant growth, it is not easy to see the birds; the open ground around the roads offers more chance of spotting the dusky Borneo Whistling Thrush and the easily identifiable Chestnut-capped Laughing Thrush.

A relatively new, alternative and somewhat tougher summit trail for climbers leaves Mesilau and eventually links up with the main summit trail at Layang-Layang, giving ambitious climbers the chance to do a circuit, leaving from Mesilau and after reaching the summit, descending to Park Headquarters.

After the dramatic landscapes of Mesilau, the warm lowland rainforest around Poring has a decidedly tropical feeling. Vast stands of thick bamboo known locally as *poring* (hence the name of the village), clumps of flowering ginger, vivid hibiscus flowers and fruit trees grow on either side of a river that separates the hot springs from the reception and information area of Poring, and the range of accommodation.

Hot mineral water gushing from the ground at Poring is channelled into baths which were originally developed by the Japanese during their occupation of Sabah in WWII. Since then, the baths have been rebuilt and include private bathing chalets as well as open-air baths. There is also a cold plunge pool known as the Rock Pool, and another freshwater pool with slides which is particularly popular with the local children.

Another of Poring's attractions is a canopy walkway strung between three giant trees in the midst of a hillside forest. From here, one can enjoy a bird's-eye view of the tree canopy, where most bird and animal activity takes place.

The walk-in butterfly garden is particularly colourful when the sun is shining, for this encourages dozens of brilliant local butterflies floating overhead. The most striking of all is the Rajah Brooke's Birdwing, a huge butterfly with iridescent green arrowhead markings on a velvet black background, contrasting with a fire-engine red thorax. The butterfly farm has a nursery and hatchery to help in conservation of native species.

Following pages: The unmistakable and powerful silhouette of Mount Kinabalu, which dominates the landscape and the legends of much of Sabah.

PHOTO BY HENRY K.Y. CHIN

Above: A dozen peaks on the summit plateau are over 3,000 m, which made it difficult for early climbers to find the true summit, Low's Peak.

PHOTO BY C.V. CHONG

—

Above right: The Sacrifice Pool, where a ritual sacrifice is held each year to appease the spirit of the mountain.

PHOTO BY C.V. CHONG

—

Opposite: Various expeditions have followed different routes to the summit, but only two have successfully managed to descend into "the dark abyss" of Low's Gully.

PHOTO BY ROBERT NEW

—

Below: Some of the most dramatic views of Mount Kinabalu can be seen from Mesilau, on the eastern side of Kinabalu Park.

PHOTO BY WENDY HUTTON

—

Above: Contented cows grazing at a dairy farm high on the eastern slopes of Mount Kinabalu, near Kundasang.
PHOTO BY C.V. CHONG

The tiny mouse-deer (not actually a member of the deer family) and full-sized local deer are housed together with colourful birds in Poring's netted Tropical Garden.

For many nature lovers, the Orchid Conservation Centre is the prime attraction at Poring, for here one can see one of Sabah's largest collections of native orchids transferred to a natural setting on a gentle hill slope. Tucked away from the other attractions of Poring, this is a place of tranquil beauty and quiet discovery.

Energetic trekkers or dedicated birdwatchers may want to take the trail that leads to the Kipungit waterfall, about 1 1/2 hours from the reception area of Poring.

Gazing at the world's largest flower, being enchanted by brilliant butterflies, spotting some remarkable birds, discovering rare native orchids, hiking a trail once used by natives carrying salt from the coast to the Interior, or simply drinking up the beauty of the virgin rainforest are some of the attractions to be found within Crocker Range National Park.

Initially designated a forest reserve in 1968, some 139,919 hectares of forested mountains were gazetted as the Crocker Range National Park in 1984. Not only does the Park possess a rich biodiversity, it receives some of Sabah's heaviest rainfall (3,000–4,000 mm annually). This makes it the prime water catchment for the entire southwestern portion of Sabah, a vital source of water for drinking, agriculture and industry for at least one-third of the state's population.

The Park (officially known as Taman Banjaran Crocker) is surrounded by communities of indigenous Kadazandusun and Murut, most of whom are agriculturalists.

The precipitous slopes of the Crocker Range are crossed by two roads from Kota Kinabalu. The major road (generally referred to as the Tambunan Road) commences in the Penampang district on the eastern outskirts of Kota Kinabalu. It climbs tortuously upwards, past small villages and the occasional makeshift stall selling fruit, vegetables or orchids.

Some of the switchback bends offer breathtaking views over forested slopes flowing like dark green waves down to the city and the blue waters of the South China Sea. Near Gunung (Mount) Alab, the road crosses Sinsuron Pass (1,649 metres) before snaking down to Tambunan, on to Keningau and to the agricultural town of Tenom (all located in the Interior District).

A second road crossing the Crocker Range begins near Kimanis, a coastal village about one-and-a-half hour's drive south of Kota Kinabalu, and leads to Keningau, the busiest town in the Interior District. Once an unsealed logging road used only by trucks heavily laden with timber from the Interior, this upgraded road climbs up to around 1,000 metres before descending to Keningau.

Above: Workers plucking the tips of tea bushes in Sabah's only tea estate, on the eastern slopes of Mount Kinabalu.

PHOTO COURTESY OF SABAH TEA

Above left: Cabbages are just one of the many varieties of temperate climate vegetables grown around Kundasang, 5 km from Kinabalu Park Headquarters.

PHOTO BY C.V. CHONG

Following pages: The rich alluvial soil brought down over the millennia by rivers arising on Mount Kinabalu is ideal for growing rice, seen here in paddy fields in Kota Belud district.

PHOTO BY HENRY K.Y. CHIN

The steep mountainsides and dense rainforest of the Park make it difficult to explore, especially as very few trails have been created by Sabah Parks (which maintains all parks within the state). However, one privately owned place on the edge of the Park provides an exceptional opportunity for discovering some of the flora and fauna of the Crocker Range. Located around 35 kilometres from Kota Kinabalu at an altitude of 800 metres, Kipandi Butterfly Park has far more than butterflies, as it is home to one of Sabah's finest private collections of native orchids, some of them extremely rare.

One of the Kadazandusun owners has been an enthusiastic collector of butterflies and beetles since boyhood. The results of his passion are evident in the insect "museum", where hundreds of butterflies, beetles, phasmids (stick insects), gloriously coloured, shiny jewel bugs and other entomological delights (some from Indonesian and Papua New Guinea) are displayed.

A huge netted butterfly enclosure has been planted with shrubs and trees which provide nectar for living butterflies. Butterflies particularly enjoy brightly coloured blooms, so scarlet ixoras, pink and orange lantana, some glorious purplish-pink flowering bananas, various gingers and hibiscus create a blaze of colour.

Above: *Dendrobium datinconnieae*, a strikingly beautiful new species described from the orchid collection cultivated at the Kipandi Butterfly Park.
PHOTO BY C.L. CHAN

—

Opposite: Waterfalls created by heavy rain make silver streaks down the granite sides of Mount Kinabalu.
PHOTO BY CH'IEN LEE

—

Following pages: Looking like a river of rocks, these granite slabs bear evidence of ice having covered the upper slopes of Mount Kinabalu during the last Ice Age.
PHOTO BY ROBERT NEW

—

Top: Hundreds of butterfly, beetle and stick insect specimens, many exquisitely beautiful, are displayed in an air-conditioned museum at Kipandi Butterfly Park.
PHOTO BY H.C. CHAN

—

Above: One of Borneo's most striking butterflies, the Rajah Brooke's Birdwing.
PHOTO BY WENDY HUTTON

—

Right: *Acriopsis javanica*, a common epiphytic orchid that has elegant inflorescences of many flowers.
PHOTO BY H.C. CHAN

—

To ensure the conservation of native species, the cocoons made by butterflies which have mated are gathered and taken into a protected area where they are monitored until the butterfly emerges. While some butterflies are kept for visitors to enjoy, the others are released into the Crocker Range Park to live freely. Some of the spectacular butterflies include the Rajah Brooke's Birdwing, with its velvet black and iridescent green markings and red thorax and head; the yellow and black Common Birdwing and the white and black Tree Nymph, which floats rather than flies through the air.

The Kipandi Butterfly Park is working with various herbaria to collect, conserve and document native orchids, and so far has over 300 species, not just from Crocker Range Park but from all of Sabah. There is a good collection of native hoyas (climbers which have clusters of waxy blooms) and an exciting collection of pitcher plants too. Memorable among these are the mountain-loving *Nepenthes lowii*, with its nipped-in waist; the handsome *N. fusca*, with its dark red neck and peristome and *N. rafflesiana*, which has in the interesting habit of growing flanges to support itself if sitting on the ground, while the aerial pitchers do not develop these.

Left: The native orchid collection at Kipandi is one of the most important in Sabah.

PHOTO BY C.L. CHAN

—

Below left: The cool, breezy slopes of the Crocker Range provide ideal growing conditions for dozens of different orchid species.

PHOTO BY C.L. CHAN

—

Below: Plants are carefully selected to provide the favourite food of the many species of butterfly bred at Kipandi.

PHOTO BY H.C. CHAN

—

Above: Despite its seemingly exotic beauty, the Bamboo Orchid can be found growing in poor soil along roadsides. This specimen, *Arundina graminifolia*, exhibits a special colour form found around the Kipandi area.

—

Right: The waxy bloom of a species of ginger (*Etlingera elatior*); the unopened buds of this flower are used in local food.

—

PHOTOS BY C.L. CHAN

Beyond Kipandi, the road towards Tambunan continues up past a few small villages or *kampung* and basic restaurants before crossing the Sinsuron Pass. From here, it is about a 5-minute drive down to the Rafflesia Forest Reserve, dedicated to the conservation of the remarkable flower first brought to world attention by Sir Stamford Raffles in 1830.

The Rafflesia Information Centre, located right beside the road, has plenty of information about this strange parasitic flower, which begins as a bud on a certain vine and takes about 8 months to reach maturity. When fully opened, the fleshy flower can measure up to 1 metre across, and gives off a pungent odour to attract pollinating flies. Many different sites where the Rafflesia blooms have been identified by the Park rangers, some of them a mere 15 minutes' walk, others as much as an hour or more away.

A hike along the Lookout Trail — even if a Rafflesia is not in bloom — is well worth taking. The altitude of around 1,000 metres makes for comfortable walking in the montane forest, where a diversity of plants including some orchids can be seen. Fortunate hikers may spot a Tufted Ground Squirrel with its magnificent long bushy tail, or the more common Bornean Mountain Ground Squirrel.

Above: A host of information about the bizarre Rafflesia is provided in the Information Centre; it is also possible to follow a trail to view any Rafflesias which may be in bloom.
PHOTO BY DR. SHAZHARN ZAIN

—

Above right: The entrance to the Rafflesia Information Centre, on the road to Tambunan, is hard to miss.
PHOTO BY DR. SHAZHARN ZAIN

—

Opposite: Squirrels such as this *Sundasciurus jentinki* (found only above 900 m in Borneo) can often be seen along the Lookout Trail in the Rafflesia Reserve.
PHOTO BY CH'IEN LEE

—

Above: This montane species, the Pale-faced Bulbul (*Pycnonotus flavescens*), is found right up to the limit of vegetation on Mount Kinabalu.

—

Above right: The Bornean Whistler (*Pachycephala hypoxantha*) is an endemic montane bird commonly found around Kinabalu Park Headquarters and as far up the trail as Paka Cave.

—

Right: The montane Sunda Bush Warbler (*Cettia vulcania*) is common in roadside scrub high on the Crocker Range, as well as within Kinabalu Park.

—

PHOTOS BY CH'IEN LEE

The forest close to the edge of the road can be rewarding for bird watchers. The small fruiting trees close to the Rafflesia Information Centre attract birds such as Sunda Laughing Thrushes and Chestnut-hooded Thrushes, as well as the endemic Mountain Barbet. Whitehead's Broadbill, the Bornean Barbet, Cinnamon-rumped Trogon, Blythe's Hawk-eagle, Red-breasted Partridge and Whitehead's Spiderhunter are all special birds which have been spotted in this location.

For an intensely rewarding experience of the Crocker Range, adventurous travellers can retrace the steps of natives from the Interior who trekked for around five days to reach the monthly market at Inobong (not far from Donggongan town). They carried with them their jungle produce, rice and tobacco, returning with their split bamboo carrying baskets loaded with metal tools, essential clothing and, above all, salt. The so-called Salt Trail can be followed today with guide and support staff. Hiking up steep, slippery slopes, fording rivers or crossing them by swaying suspension bridge, camping and staying in a native village home are all part of the adventure.

Few visitors explore the Crocker Range Park from the Kimanis–Keningau Road, yet it offers a convenient base with accommodation and an information centre just 12 kilometres from Keningau. The road from Kimanis crosses flat agricultural land with a few Kadazandusun villages before starting its very steep climb up the mountains. Most of the land close to the road is unfortunately outside the Park boundaries, yet the somewhat degraded vegetation still provides bird watchers with the opportunity to spot a Mountain Imperial Pigeon perching in a giant tree or a soaring eagle.

Above left: The tiny, jewel-bright Pygmy Blue Flycatcher (*Muscicapella hodgsoni*) is a rare montane species.

—

Above: At first glance very similar to the Pygmy Blue Flycatcher, this Snowy-browed Flycatcher (*Ficedula hyperythra*) has a distinctive white "eyebrow". It is a very common resident of the forest understorey on Kinabalu and the Crocker Range.

—

PHOTOS BY CH'IEN LEE

Above: The Indigo Flycatcher (*Eumyias indigo*) is a common and surprisingly tame resident of the forest around Kinabalu Park Headquarters.

—

Above right: This busy little insect eater, the Mountain Leaf-Warbler (*Phylloscopus trivirgatus*), is the bird most frequently encountered along the Summit Trail of Mount Kinabalu.

—

Opposite: A very noisy bird, the Chestnut-hooded Laughing-thrush (*Rhinocichla treacheri*) is easily heard and seen in mountainous regions of Borneo. It can often be spotted feeding on insects on the lawns, and feasting on fruits and berries around Kinabalu Park Headquarters.

—

PHOTOS BY CH'IEN LEE

Perhaps the best place in all of Sabah for an unobstructed view of endless hills covered with virgin rainforest can be enjoyed once across the pass. The Crocker Range Park Keningau Head-Station is an ideal spot to spend a night, with accommodation (dormitory or private rooms) and cooking facilities, an information centre and a trail that runs behind the station. There is a Rafflesia site along this trail, and although some of the forest here has been disturbed in the past for agriculture, it still offers a glimpse of the flora and fauna of the Park.

Bird watchers interested in endemic species (those found only in north Borneo) will find an early morning outing along the road between the station and the pass rewarding. As the morning mist lies like a veil across some of the giant dipterocarp trees in the forest, the ringing call of the Great Argus Pheasant can often be heard rising from the valleys. The endemic Golden-naped Barbet can often be heard, although it is difficult to spot. Hornbills can often be seen, especially if there happens to be a fruiting fig tree in the vicinity.

The world's tiniest raptor, the endemic White-fronted Falconet, can often be seen in the early morning, perching on a tall dead branch not far from the road edge. Later in the day, one or two falconets can often be seen sitting in a pine tree in the grounds of the Sabah Parks station, waiting to make a kill.

7.

Where the Wild Things are

Slender white egrets poise nonchalantly on long spindly legs at the edge of a busy traffic roundabout, while not far away, a giant tree dripping with clusters of lush ferns throws a vast net of shade over the cars parked outside a busy downtown bank. A chaotic tumble of green clings to the steep sides of Signal Hill, overlooking the old centre of Kota Kinabalu, and macaques are sometimes seen along the roadside not far from the Istana or Governor's Palace. Massive whale sharks are usually spotted feeding on krill each February or March in the waters of Gaya Bay, and turtles still raise their heads for a gulp of air beside surprised snorkellers in the Tunku Abdul Rahman Marine Park.

Sabah has become known for its large rainforest sanctuaries including Danum Valley Conservation Area and Tabin Wildlife Reserve, and the remarkable patches of forest along the banks of the Kinabatangan River on Sabah's east coast. However, Kota Kinabalu — which bills itself as the Rainforest City — is blessed with a surprising amount of plant and animal life. One does not have to go far afield to see many of the natural wonders of Borneo.

The endemic Proboscis Monkey lives in freshwater swamps in a few parts of Borneo; nowhere else in the world can you see this bizarre and beautifully coloured creature in the wild, the male endowed with a great pot belly and dangling fleshy noise. Small groups of these monkeys can be seen just a couple of hours from Kota Kinabalu, along the rivers of the Klias Peninsula near Beaufort.

Opposite: Egrets (the official birds of Kota Kinabalu) are one of the most common birds seen around the city, not just near the lagoons and wetlands but even at the side of city streets.

PHOTO BY HENRY K.Y. CHIN

—

Following pages: A group of female and juvenile Proboscis Monkeys, guarded by a dominant male, gather in a tree at dusk alongside the Klias River south of Kota Kinabalu.

PHOTO BY CH'IEN LEE

—

Above: A male Proboscis Monkey, with that unmistakable nose, honks down to warn off anyone or anything that he finds threatening.
PHOTO BY A.Y.C. CHUNG

—

Above right: A boatload of visitors heads down a canal towards the Garama River for wildlife viewing in the Klias Peninsula.
PHOTO BY WENDY HUTTON

—

Opposite: Vast areas of peat swamp forest and other wetlands have been drained, much of the original vegetation replaced by oil palm and other crops. Clumps of sago palm (once providing the local staple, sago starch) can still be found in areas such as this.
PHOTO BY WENDY HUTTON

—

Proboscis Monkeys — which have pale reddish and grey coats, white "underpants" and a bright white tail — normally live in groups, the females and their young watched over jealously by an alpha male. Troops of younger males (the "bachelors") also live in groups, keeping an eye out for an opportunity to usurp the dominant male and take over his harem. The monkeys always congregate in trees along a river bank in the late afternoon, enjoying a few last leaves for the day, socialising or fighting before settling down to sleep.

This habit makes it easy for visitors travelling slowly along the rivers to stop and be entertained by the behaviour of the Proboscis Monkeys in the nearby trees, to look at the swamp forest and to keep an eye out for the rare Silver Leaf Monkey, flying foxes and birds, particularly kingfishers. In addition, it is possible to see literally hundreds of water buffaloes congregating in the swamps at the edge of the Garama River at dusk.

Afternoon river safaris leave from two main centres in the Klias Peninsula: near the village of Kota Klias and from Garama, further towards the Brunei Bay side of the peninsula. (Tours normally return to Kota Kinabalu the same evening.)

Proboscis Monkeys can also be seen around Weston, where it is also possible to cruise through the beautiful *nipah* swamp forests in the estuary of the Padas River, flowing out into Brunei Bay.

Above: A little train provides entertainment for the children and a chance for older visitors to relax as they tour around the Lok Kawi Wildlife Park.
PHOTO BY PEIN LEE/STB

—

Above right: A Malayan Sun Bear shows its amazingly long tongue.
PHOTO BY PEIN LEE/STB

—

Right: A female Sumatran Rhinoceros, past breeding age; this species is highly endangered as a result of poaching and habitat loss.
PHOTO BY WENDY HUTTON

—

Where the Wild Things are

Although wonderful birds, macaques, squirrels and other small mammals can be spotted in the wild or in protected parks near Kota Kinabalu, the closest place to discover a wide range of Sabah's animals and birds is the Lok Kawi Wildlife Park. Opened in 2007 and managed by the Sabah Wildlife Department, the Park consists of a zoo plus a botanical trail that allows visitors to enjoy the flora as well as the fauna.

Located in a small valley in a semi-rural area less than 30 minutes from the city, the Wildlife Park is home to more than 100 animals yet is not so large as to be tiring to explore. Indeed, beautiful vegetation, shady pathways, rest stops and refreshment areas make it a pleasure to wander about.

Some of Sabah's rarest animals can be found here, including the critically endangered Sumatran or Asian One-horned Rhinoceros. Currently the focus of a captive breeding programme in Tabin Wildlife Reserve on Sabah's east coast, this is the world's smallest rhino and as few as 30–50 of the Bornean sub-species are believed to still live in the wild in Sabah. (They have disappeared elsewhere in Borneo owing to poaching for their horn and to loss of habitat.)

The elephant enclosure, with its large bathing pool, is where the world's smallest elephant, the Bornean Pygmy Elephant, can be found. The fact that these animals (which had already been living in captivity before coming to Lok Kawi) have produced babies is a sign that they are happy in their new home. A small population of elephants still lives in the wild in eastern Sabah, along the Kinabatangan River, in Danum Valley and in Tabin.

The Wildlife Park's small group of Proboscis Monkeys, notoriously difficult to keep in captivity, have also adjusted well and even produced babies. Another fascinating primate found here is the Bornean Gibbon, a restless, long-armed furry creature which swings from branch to branch with the most incredible speed.

Sabah's icon, the red-haired and gentle Orangutan, is an incredibly strong and intelligent creature. Visitors to the daily Animal Show are invariably amused and amazed in equal proportions by the Wildlife Park's Orangutans, especially their speed at opening a coconut.

Among the many other animals are the Malayan Sun Bear, two species of deer and the handsome Malayan Tiger (found only in Peninsular Malaysia and not on Borneo). And to keep younger visitors happy, there is a dedicated Children's Zoo.

Birds kept in netted aviaries greet visitors right near the entrance to the Wildlife Park, with several Hill Mynahs (which are brilliant mimics) calling out the Muslim greeting "Salam Aleikum", trying their skill at English with an "Hello" or even muttering in Chinese. Some interesting owls, including the large-eyed Buffy Fish Owl, can be seen here too.

However, the most enchanting area for bird lovers is the huge, walk-in aviary — a natural river valley covered by high netting. Apart from more talkative mynahs,

Above: The Orangutans are among the most popular animals at Lok Kawi, especially when performing in the daily Animal Show.

—

Following pages: The Kota Kinabalu Wetland Centre at Likas, with boardwalks, shady rest areas and a bird hide, is less than 2 km from the city centre.

—

PHOTOS BY PEIN LEE/STB

Top: This self-confident bird, a Hill Mynah, is remarkably clever at mimicking humans.

—

Above: A Wandering Whistling Duck (*Dendrocygna arcuata*), one of the many feathered residents of the large walk-in aviary at Lok Kawi.

—

Right: The Striated Heron (*Butorides striata*), the most common heron in Sabah, characteristically stands absolutely still as it waits for its food to swim past.

—

PHOTOS BY WENDY HUTTON

there are also blue and white Black-crowned Night Herons wading in the river, perhaps with a beautifully coloured Wandering Whistling-Duck nearby. The glorious glossy black Prevost's Squirrel with its bright orange belly can sometimes be spotted stealing pieces of papaya left out for birds such as a pair of snowy white Pied Imperial Pigeons, with contrasting black underwings and tail.

Bird lovers will find top birding destinations such as Kinabalu Park and other areas of Crocker Range richly rewarding (see previous chapter). However, just a couple of kilometres from the centre of Kota Kinabalu, a 24-hectare mangrove forest is home to almost 80 species of resident and migratory birds.

Once known as the Kota Kinabalu Bird Sanctuary, this has been renamed the Kota Kinabalu Wetland Centre. From wooden boardwalks over the swamp, it is possible to see the blue and white Collared Kingfisher, or the less common Stork-billed Kingfisher with its large bright orange beak. Egrets and herons can be seen year round, and during the winter months of northern Asia and Siberia, migratory species such as the Marsh Sandpiper, the red-legged Common Redshank and the Common Greenshank can be observed.

The Likas Lagoon, on one side of the coastal road at the edge of Likas Bay, is a popular feeding sight for egrets, and at times, dozens of them can be seen in the shallow waters — totally unconcerned by passing traffic.

Where the Wild Things are

Tropical rainforest can be enjoyed on the islands of Tunku Abdul Rahman Park, especially Pulau Gaya, close to Kota Kinabalu, as well as further afield in the Crocker Range and Kinabalu Park. However, it is also possible to see some of Borneo's most beautiful plants such as orchids just on the outskirts of Kota Kinabalu.

Orchids embody the extravagant beauty of tropical flowers, yet surprisingly, they are the world's most varied plant species and grow around the world. Nonetheless, tropical orchids (and particularly those of Borneo) are among the most fascinating and lovely of all flowers.

Right in the heart of Kota Kinabalu, there is an impressive display of local and imported plants each Sunday morning at the Gaya Street Fair. Because of strict controls to ensure conservation of native species, the many orchids on sale here are hybrids, grown for their beauty and destined to finish up in the collection of Sabah's many local orchid lovers.

As well as the orchids, local fruit trees, spectacular palms, brilliant bougainvillea, hibiscus in all colours and aquatic plants are among the many plants on display here.

Below: The Likas Sports Complex offers a wide range of activities including swimming (the covered Olympic-sized pool can be seen in the background), with a man-made lake followed by a trail idea for strolling or jogging.

PHOTO BY LEE YEN PHIN

8.

Borneo Adventures

The north of Borneo seems to have been made for adventure. Whatever your sport — racing through the rapids in an inflatable raft or making a roped climb high on a cliff face on Mount Kinabalu, scuba diving around a coral reef or enjoying a leisurely game of golf — Kota Kinabalu and its environs offer something for everyone.

With its year-round summer and warm seas, this is the perfect place for all kinds of water sports. Lazing in the sea just off a beach is a great way to enjoy the tropical climate, but don a mask and snorkel and a pair of fins and a whole new world is revealed. Tiny vividly coloured reef fish dart in and out of nooks and crannies, clown fish (Nemo, no less) guard the sea anemones which protect them from predators, intricately patterned and coloured hard corals and waving soft corals are all there just below the surface of the sea.

Reefs off the islands of the Tunku Abdul Rahman Park, particularly Sulug, Mamutik and Sapi, are enchanting places to snorkel, and all the equipment you need can be rented either from a tour operator or on the island (except for Pulau Sulug). Those who want a closer view of the underwater world but who are not ready to try scuba diving might find "sea walking" easier. With the help of a special diving helmet which receives air via a hose to the surface, and with a guide leading the way on the sea floor past a reef just off Pulau Gaya, this is a novel approach to underwater exploration. Another unusual way of seeing below the surface is on a special underwater scooter which can be rented on Pulau Mamutik.

Various water sports such as parasailing, skimming the waves in a dinghy or Hobie-cat, paddling a kayaking or riding a huge inflated "banana" towed by a

Opposite: Parasailors near the coast of Kota Kinabalu are treated to a view of the circular Menara Tun Mustapha, home to the Sabah Foundation or Yayasan Sabah.

PHOTO BY C.V. CHONG

—

Following pages: Yachts off Tanjung Aru competing in an annual international yachting regatta.

PHOTO BY LEE YEN PHIN

—

TUATARA
TUATARA

Top: Riding an inflatable raft resembling several bananas joined together is harder than it looks, but provides loads of fun. PHOTO BY DAVID KIRKLAND/STB
Above: When the winds are up, the windsurfers are out. PHOTO BY HENRY K.Y. CHIN

Top left: The lack of strong currents in the waters around Tunku Abdul Rahman Park makes this an ideal spot for diver training.
PHOTO BY MATT OLDFIELD/SCUBAZOO

Below left: A surfacing diver's-eye view of the jetty at Pulau Mamutik.
PHOTO BY JASON ISLEY/SCUBAZOO

Above: Going down! A scuba diver takes a giant stride into the South China Sea.
PHOTO BY JASON ISLEY/SCUBAZOO

speedboat are offered by 5-star resorts in Kota Kinabalu as well as along the coast at Karambunai and Pantai Dalit. In addition, a modest development between the mangroves and the long Tuaran beach offers adventurous visitors the opportunity to kayak in local wooden canoes, to ride quad bikes along the beach, to try catching crabs and finish off a day of adventure by camping under the stars.

Sabah's prime scuba diving sites off the east coast are world renowned, but Kota Kinabalu has a lot to offer, especially for learner divers. The reefs around the islands of Pulau Mamutik, Pulau Sapi and Pulau Sulug are shallow, and protected from the open ocean. Furthermore, there are no strong currents, all of which make Kota Kinabalu an ideal place to learn to dive. Several dive operators (including Sabah Divers and Borneo Divers) offer training, as well as open-water dives for certified divers, at sites a mere 15–20 minutes by boat from Kota Kinabalu.

Although there are coral reefs off Pulau Tiga, south of Kota Kinabalu, prevailing winds and currents normally limit visibility. Better diving can usually be enjoyed at Mantanani, a (long) day trip from the city via Kota Belud. At least 20 dive sites have been identified here and this dive location is known for its colourful nudibranchs and occasional visits from the rare dugong or sea cow.

Following pages: Colourful reef fish swim among the corals of the reefs off Pulau Sapi, Mamutik and Sulug, only minutes from downtown Kota Kinabalu.
PHOTO BY JASON ISLEY/SCUBAZOO

Above and above right: White-water rafting in Sabah began in the Padas river, where the more challenging rapids make it ideal for the adventurous and experienced.

—

PHOTOS BY WENDY HUTTON

Move inland and there's still plenty of water to provide fun and adventure. Rivers are a great place to picnic and cool off, but add a strong inflatable boat, plenty of boulders, a few rapids, scenic villages and areas of forested hillside and they become an exciting venue for white-water rafting.

This sport was first established in Sabah along the west coast's biggest river, the Padas, which rises high in the mountains of the southwest and flows down across the valley of Tenom, through a narrow river gorge past Beaufort and then on out to Brunei Bay. To reach the tiny settlement of Panggi where the rafting begins, it is necessary to travel about 1 1/2 hours by road to Beaufort, then to take a train or railcar along the narrow Padas gorge where the river fights its way to the coast around huge boulders, with calmer stretches where it ripples over shingle beds. The Padas can offer an exciting challenge which serious rafters are happy to opt for, despite the long travel to and from the rafting location.

For others who want a less challenging and even more scenic experience, as well as one that is closer to Kota Kinabalu, the lovely Kiulu River is the perfect solution. Fed by streams that run down from the Crocker Range, the Kiulu River eventually flows past the town of Tamparuli and on to the Tuaran River. It is only 1 1/2 hours by tour bus from Kota Kinabalu to the start point for rafting, and the descent by raft takes about the same time, depending upon the amount of water in the river. After sustained heavy rains, the river moves at an impressive pace, though most of the time, the 14-kilometre journey takes a leisurely 1 1/2 hours of fun that is safe for all, including young children.

Typical local suspension bridges are strung across the river, linking villages to fertile riverside fields or to other small settlements. Towering stands of bamboo, fruit trees and palms crowd the banks for much of the rafting journey, which finishes for most at a riverside lodge with showers and a barbecue lunch to satisfy the ravenous appetite built up by this spot of adventure.

Above: The Nature Interpretation Centre and a suspension bridge leading to a site for young orangutans being trained to return to the wild are part of Rasa Ria's Nature Reserve, on one edge of the resort. PHOTOS COURTESY BY SHANGRI-LA'S RASA RIA RESORT

Above: Long sandy beaches in the Tuaran district are ideal for horse-riding, which is offered by a couple of resorts.

PHOTO COURTESY OF SHANGRI-LA'S RASA RIA RESORT

—

Another way to enjoy the uncrowded environment of the countryside around Kota Kinabalu is to go horse-riding; with mile after mile of unspoiled beaches, the west coast is ideal for this sport. Although horses are not native to Borneo, they have been here a long time and a small breed of local pony is still used as a means of transport by some Bajau people in the Kota Belud district. Horse-racing, too, is a popular sport and takes place at a race-course in the Tuaran district every weekend.

There are stables at a couple of 5-star resorts some 30–40 minutes north of the city, at Karambunai and Pantai Dalit. A little further north, at Tuaran Beach, another resort has Sabah's largest private stable of experienced horses at its Kindawan Riding Centre. As well as long beach rides, it is possible to ride through a nearby village and see the lifestyle of the local Bajaus, or to ride along the edge of wetlands and view the mangrove habitat.

In the past decade, mountain biking has become very popular in Sabah's west coast district. Apart from annual adventure challenges which feature tough mountain biking, or combine mountain biking with other sporting disciplines, there are many other options for those who enjoy a physical challenge. From the seat of a bicycle, the surrounding countryside becomes a lot more of a sensory experience compared with travelling by vehicle. The cyclist hears, smells and sees things that others miss, and stopping at a roadside stall or a remote village is sure to result in contact with curious and friendly locals.

The relatively flat land around Penampang on Kota Kinabalu's outskirts, and the attractive rural surroundings south at Papar make these areas ideal for day trips by mountain bike. Another popular spot combining a look at the local culture (in this case, that of the Bajau tribe) with cycling is in Kota Belud district. For more of a challenge, adventure tourism operators take cyclists to the hills behind Telipok, or up the Kiulu valley. For the really tough, cycling high on the Crocker Range near Kota Kinabalu, on steep slopes around Kampung Kiau or Kampung Kaung, or on the eastern slopes of the mountain near Mount Kinabalu Golf Club, are some of the options.

Trips involving overnight camping or staying in a village sometimes include a refreshing dip at a waterfall or finish with a white-water rafting trip on the Kiulu or Padas rivers. Depending on the location, cyclists follow regular roads or forestry roads, or ride along simple tracks through the forest.

Those who prefer an engine to do the work when they're riding on a bike will find a Kota Kinabalu-based company devoted to biking adventures in Sabah. Bikers ride 650 cc motor bikes to explore some of the most scenic and sometimes almost deserted countryside, leaving the home base in a luxurious house high on the Crocker Range and travelling north to Kudat, across to Mount Kinabalu or on to Sandakan on the east coast.

The bikers are accompanied by a well-equipped back-up crew, and overnight stops are made in superbly comfortable private homes or fine hotels, with food to match. Some might call it soft adventure, but those who prefer it when the going gets rough can opt for biking on gravel routes in more rugged environments.

The challenging nature of much of the countryside around Kota Kinabalu, combined with a humid tropical climate, means that trekking can be a surprisingly tiring activity.

Below: Quad bikes provide enormous fun for holiday makers.

PHOTO COURTESY OF SHANGRI-LA'S RASA RIA RESORT

Without doubt, the most popular trek in Sabah is the summit trail of Mount Kinabalu. The main trail leaves from Timpohon Gate near Park Headquarters, with most climbers taking around 5–6 hours to reach Panar Laban where they stay for the night. The following morning, an early departure for the final 2-hour climb to the summit sees most trekkers more than 4,000 metres high, on the summit plateau of Mount Kinabalu.

An alternative, tougher and longer trail leaves from Mesilau on the Park's eastern side; 4.5 km later, this meets up with the main summit trail at Layang Layang, with another 2–3 hours of climbing.

There are plenty of other trails which have become popular with hikers who want a trip which is not only challenging but offers some insight into local culture. One such trek follows the trail once used by Dusuns from the Interior, who carried huge backpacks of rice and other produce for at least five days, as they crossed over the mountains of the Crocker Range to come down to the monthly market of Inobong in the Penampang district. They returned with salt, as well as manufactured goods, giving this route the name "the salt trail". Several adventure tour operators organise the logistics of this and similar treks, including staying for at least one night in an isolated local village.

Exploring one of the many forest reserves or Parks near Kota Kinabalu invariably involves hiking, even if only for an hour or so. However, although there is plenty of opportunity for a good work-out along trails in the Rafflesia Reserve and Kinabalu Park, the fascination of the vegetation, the birds and the many fascinating insects is almost certain to result in frequent pauses.

Although a small number of local enthusiasts meet each Sunday morning to scale rock walls at Kirongu in Inanam district, rock climbing is a new sport in Sabah. It was given a big boost in 2007 with the establishment of rock climbing with handrails, ladders, cables and life lines more than 3,000 metres above sea level on Mount Kinabalu.

Referred to as a *via ferrata* (Italian for 'fully equipped route'), Mountain Torq's *via ferrata* is a trail marked by iron rungs, footholds, cables and rails wrapped around the mountain's northeast face. Designed for the fit and adventurous, this *via ferrata* is sure to give an entirely new perspective to Mount Kinabalu. Mountain Torq also provides introductory and advanced courses in sports climbing, abseiling and rope ascending.

Opposite: Getting up close and personal with The Mountain; climbers enjoying the challenges of Kinabalu's Mountain Torq.
PHOTO COURTESY OF MOUNTAIN TORQ

Below: The reward for skilful climbers is stunning views down over the lower slopes of the Crocker Range.
PHOTO COURTESY OF MOUNTAIN TORQ

Following pages: The Dalit Bay Golf and Country Club, adjacent to Shangri-la's Rasa Ria Resort, offers areas of wetland and a hole that stretches along a river.
PHOTO BY PEIN LEE/STB

Above: Located just minutes from downtown, the 27-hole golf course at Sutera Harbour is the only one open during the cooler hours of evening.
PHOTO BY JASON ISLEY/SCUBAZOO
—

With 6 golf courses located in or near Kota Kinabalu, this is a golfer's heaven. For a start — and vitally important for most golfers — the courses offer a superb range of natural surroundings, which always provide one of the main pleasures of the game. There are designer courses near the sea, some with natural freshwater features or swamps; other courses with a city backdrop; tranquil fairways meandering over the hills and others high on a mountain slope where the ball might disappear in a sudden cloud.

There is a magnificent 27-hole course designed by Graham Marsh at Sutera Harbour, right in Kota Kinabalu and just 10 minutes from the airport. A gracious golf and country club with Sabah's oldest 18-hole course is only 10 minutes' drive from the city centre, and offers attractive hilly terrain with mature trees. The city's oldest course is the 9-hole links located right by Tanjung Aru beach, giving the city a total of 3 golf courses.

For those who love to play golf near the sea, there are another two 18-hole courses located next to 5-star resorts less than an hour north of the city, one at Karambunai and

the other at Pantai Dalit. Both courses offer a mixture of terrain (plus, on occasion, ocean breezes which add another element to the game). A little over an hour south of the city, at Bongawan, is a Jack Nicklaus-designed 18-hole course located right on the beach, with an adjacent resort hotel.

Sabah's highest golf course is located at 1,500 metres, not far from Mesilau on the Pinosuk Plateau on the eastern slopes of Mount Kinabalu. With stunning views over farmlands and the endless green hills of the Crocker Range, this is a place where it's easy to take your eye off the ball. The 18-hole course has jokingly been described as 9 holes up the mountainside and 9 holes down, and it's true that it is challenging both physically and mentally.

Almost all these golf courses offer excellent facilities with clubhouses complete with changing room, restaurant and lounge; practice putting, chipping, driving and bunker areas; pro shop; caddy service and for those who have come unprepared, all necessary equipment for rental.

Above: The 11th hole at the Dalit Bay Golf and Country Club has an unusual potential hazard: distracting views of one of Sabah's icons.
PHOTO BY DAVID KIRKLAND/STB